# Leave the Silver
# & Choose Gold!

CHARMAIN LIVINGSTON

Order this book online at www.trafford.com
or email orders@trafford.com

Most Trafford titles are also available at major online book retailers.

Printed in the United States of America.

ISBN: 978-1-4120-5569-7 (sc)


*Trafford rev. 03/18/2011*

  www.trafford.com

**North America & international**
toll-free: 1 888 232 4444 (USA & Canada)
phone: 250 383 6864 ♦ fax: 812 355 4082

When I first started writing this book about 5 years ago, it was entitled "when is daddy coming home". This was a question constantly asked by my young girls at that time. As the months went on continuing to write the book and after my deliverance came, the Holy Spirit impressed upon my heart to change the name of the book to 'Leave the Silver and Choose Gold'.

I dedicate this book to my two daughters, Stephanie and Vanessa who have been my inspiration, and tower of strength in a time of much desperation and determination to see the promise of God become real and tangible in our lives.

I love you both very much and I hope that you both will one day, be able to share with other children the Joy of the Lord, and lead others into His presence to seek

His strength, especially when there is no 'father figure' in the home.

I would also like to dedicate this book to all single parents who by unforeseen circumstances have been forced to nurture and bring up their children alone, without the valuable time and effort of a father in their very young lives. Know that God is with you always, watching over you and your children. Your children are a gift from God to you, they are your most valuable treasure besides God, and if you plant in them the word of God they will bear fruit and glorify the name of the Lord!

A special thank you to God for His Grace and Mercy and for His Faithfulness, who without the ministry of the Holy Spirit, I could never have completed this book and testimony.

# CONTENTS

## INTRODUCTION

There is no other way for the *promises* of God to come to you except for your **OBEDIENCE** to His instructions.

I encourage and beseech you, please, read the book of Deuteronomy and let the word '*obedience*' sink deep down into the depths of your *spirit*, heart and belly. Let it get into the spirit of your mind so that you move *when* God tells you to and *how* God tells you to move.

**Gold** represents perseverance, endurance, trust, love, patience, understanding and what God has ordained for us to have in our lives. God's choice for us may not always be our initial choice, but when you realise that you were placed on the earth for such a time as this, you will come to the realisation that your life is not your own. Jesus is living His life through you, and you are the *special* vessel that He has chosen to use for His purposes and for His glory, then you will understand that you have to leave your plans, goals and ambitions in order to attain the Christ in you, the *hope of glory!*.

**Silver** represents our wrong choices, carnal choices that do not coincide with the will of God for our lives. When we allow God to only half purge us and half purify us in the fire, then we resist the promises of God becoming manifested and a reality in our lives.

God never intended for us to remain in the valley, only pass through and bring out the testimony of God. The valley is preparing us to go to the next level and experience the glory of God.

God never intended for us to remain in the wilderness, just pass through and prepare us for the promise land, where we enter into our *REST*.

Has God made you a specific promise? Well do not settle for second best. This is your *moment;* this is your hour to come into the full and real blessings of God.

Don't get tired *get radical*. God is with you to accomplish and fulfil the will of God in your life, if you will wage a good warfare, through your obedience in what He tells you to do.

Choose gold, obedience, God's way and live or choose silver, your way, disobedience and suffer the consequences.

Prayer: Lord give us a taste for GOLD, for your will, for the new things of God that you have already prepared for us from before the foundation of the world. Let the old become inciped in our mouths and hearts, so that we reach out with a passion, for the new thing that God is doing in our lives. Old things are passed away and *behold* all things are become new when you are in Christ Jesus. Magnify your holy name in our lives Lord, for your glory, honour and praise. Make your holy Name great in our lives, through Jesus Christ your Son. I ask this in the Name of Jesus, the name that is above every other name. AMEN!

# CHAPTER 1

## CHOOSE LIFE!

It was the summer of June 1992, when my now ex partner of ten years came home and said 'I will be going to my parents for a couple of weeks'. I said 'okay', thinking that at last we would be able to sort out our personal problems with some distance between us. Well, to my surprise at the time, he never returned and a few months later it began to sink in, that we had been abandoned and he was gone for good.

During the last two years of the relationship I started to go to Church. There was a longing in my heart for God. All of a sudden everything I had was no longer enough or pleasing to me because I had this desire within me for God. I could not figure out how I was going to give my life back to the Lord, when I was living in sin with a man I was not married to and with two children. I wanted so desperately to return to God and be married to their father so that I could get on with serving the Lord. I felt totally ashamed of my condition and didn't know what to do about it.

I started a period of fasting and prayer, *in my condition*, on and off and of course nothing happened. So when he finally left 2 years after I started visiting Church, I figured this was actually God's answer to my prayer for marriage, and later on I found it hard to cope with.

I went to Church as usual on a Sunday night and found comfort in the presence of the Lord. But soon enough the adversary Satan said, you have not done enough yet and there are still some things you need to try out before you completely give your life to the Lord. I surrendered to the devil's lies and decided that I wouldn't be in such a hurry to get saved just yet.

I continued to send the children to Sunday School. Now and again I would go in the evenings. I found that if I did not go, I would have a really hard week so I eventually learned to just keep going without making any real commitment to the Lord.

Until one Sunday in September 1994, I decided that enough is enough. It became obvious to me that the devil had a plan for my life, but God has a better and greater plan. I had been listening to some tapes on the Nation of Islam religion as the father of my children had by now become a muslim and had been giving me literature to read and watch hoping I would get converted to his new found religion. I would fall into a heavy sleep whilst trying to watch the videos and when reading the books my spirit just rejected everything I read. I could not digest it in any way and I know now that was the Lord protecting me from being drawn further into the kingdom of darkness.

Every Sunday morning I would rise up early and watch the Christian teachings on the B.E.T. channel through cable television when it first started. At that time Pastor Frederick Price and Pastor Creflo Dollar taught for one hour each and I would tape their programme and watch it over and over again during the week. This came just in time as had it not been for the bible teachings of these two men getting into my spirit, the enemy would have found room to place in me his false teachings and who knows where I would have been today!

Pastor Dollar taught a series on 'Reconciliation with Christ' which is what really was the final push that I needed to return to the Lord. I was living in condemnation and guilt and couldn't get free from it until I heard the teaching on 'reconciliation'. I praise God for these men of God who were obedient to God preaching and teaching the Gospel of Jesus Christ on Television.

One Sunday morning I was preparing our West Indian traditional 'Sunday dinner', rice and peas and chicken. At the same time I was listening to the teachings on 'reconciliation'. I don't know what really happened, and I can't explain it but something happened. All of a sudden I switched off the cooker, left the food half cooked, ran upstairs and got ready to go to Church and called my sister to pick me up on her way. I can tell you that I have been going ever since. That day I made a conscious decision and made up in my mind that I would serve God. My grandmother used to say to me, 'Charmain, you have to *make up in your mind* to serve God and *have* a *made up mind*'. I secretly thought about this many times.

I repented in my heart and God turned me towards Him and I have not looked back since because I know and am assured in my heart, that there is nothing to go back to. Praise God I have no regrets either. Jesus is the best thing that could ever happen to me and my only wish is that I had given up the struggle long ago and surrendered my life to Him. I had made the right choice to serve the Lord.

Still, there is a time and a purpose for every thing. Nothing happens before the time. So there is no need to feel guilty about where you are now, just convicted. Keep on going to Church and believing in His word that He will bring you out, and your day of victory will come. Trust in the Lord, and believe in His Word. Put your hope in Jesus, put your faith in Jesus and Him alone for the arm of flesh *will* fail you.

**Bread or Stone, Silver or Gold**

*'Or what man is there of you, whom if his son ask bread, will he give him a stone? Or if he ask a fish, will he give him a serpent?*

*If ye then, being evil, know how to give good gifts unto your children, how much more shall your Father which is in heaven give good things to them that ask him?*

Matthew 7:9-11

Many times we are praying and asking God for things that we feel we need that are not in God's divine will for our lives, this is *stone*. It is important to pray the divine will of God into our lives, otherwise we are praying amiss! You will only know His divine will when you seek His face and He deposits His will and desires for you, into your spirit and heart, then you can pray effectively because you have received bread from heaven.

> *"I Am the living bread of life which cometh down from Heaven",*
>
> St. John 6:51.

Christ is the bread of life that came down from Heaven and in Him there is LIFE. Therefore the bread can be seen as having nutritious ingredients, and is good for a healthy spiritual diet. It has good quality ingredients. It will be satisfying, edifying, beneficial, strengthening and bring healing to us spiritually and mentally, affecting our emotional, spiritual and physical being. Bread is symbolic of provision, God has promised to supply all our needs according to His riches in glory. If received on a regular basis it will eventually cause us to enjoy restoration in every area of our lives.

On the other hand 'stone' is not edible or tasteful and is extremely hard. Nor has it any nutritious ingredients. Therefore, why should you want to consume that which is not consumable, edible or beneficial to you in any way? This is not what God would choose for you either.

We would not give our sons and daughters stones to eat, or buy things for them that is not going be productive or beneficial to them in any way. As the parent we see further than they do and know what is good or bad for them. So it is with God. We ask God for the things that we see with the natural eye, having no revelation or true understanding of it's real content. If you tried to bite stone, your teeth would break. Realise then, that it is not God's will for us to have things or persons in our lives that are not being profitable and edifying to us. It's God's will to prosper us and to give us an expected end and to have us succeed and excel to our highest potential!

In Exodus chapter 2, we read about Moses fleeing from Egypt because he murdered an Egyptian and now feared for his life. Moses fled for his life and it would seem that he did not have time to even pack a bag. He was driven by his fear into the wilderness. He arrives in Midian tired, weary, discouraged and worn out but it was at this crucial point that as he sat down by a 'certain well', his life was about to take a roundabout turn. His needs were about to be met in every way.

**The Well**

A well is a consistent supply of water preserving human life or provision. It can also be a supply of gas and oil and we know that in the scriptures fire, oil and water is symbolic of the Holy Spirit. The three are one because they each refer to aspects of *life, and* life relates to the Father, Son and Holy Spirit. All life comes from God.

The Well relates to comfort, wealth, prosperity and hope. Moses is sitting by the well and from a distance he observes the situation at hand. The shepherdesses are trying to give water to their flock, but the other shepherds intimidate and hinder them in their work feeding the sheep. As Moses watches the injustice that is being done to these women who are *uncovered* and *unprotected* without the presence and influence of a male counterpart. Moses is moved with compassion once *again* for the women as they are being mocked and finally he **stood up**! Moses put his troubles and fears aside and saw the need of someone else. He saw past his pain and present condition and arose to the challenge and seized the opportunity to deliver these women out of a terrible humiliating experience, which had probably been going on for some time.

Moses intervened again in an argument that was no business of his but *this time* the response was different. Moses steps in and assists them in giving water to their sheep and for once they arrive home early to their father who is alarmed at their quick return. *Their help had come from the Lord, through Moses.* Exodus 2:11-21

Their father Jethro tells them to call for the man who helped his daughters and invites him to come into his home, sit down with them and 'eat bread'. The bread had all the nutritious ingredients that Moses required. Through making the right choice and accepting the invitation, he received not only bread or an evening meal, but Moses ended up with a home and a new family, a job and a wife. His whole life's needs were taken care of at this *one place*. Here Moses found his purpose for this new time and season of his life. Moses received *'bread from heaven'*, provision for 'God's vision, the Father's vision for his life. Wow!

When you are in your rightful place, God will release the *'bread'* that He has for you. The provision or the blessings of the Lord came to Moses and he did not have to strive for this, it was all pre-planned and pre-ordained by God. He should have been going to a prison cell or to the death chamber because he had just committed murder. It wasn't a palace like where he used to live but this was the grace and mercy and favour of God. God sustained him and released a flow of blessings in his life. This is *'the place'* where God desired for Moses to be in order to prepare him for the next dimension of his life. A place of rest, for his weary soul. He was to feed and protect the sheep of his father-in-law Jethro, after which he was destined to lead millions of God's people, the children of Israel, out of captivity into freedom. This was to be a time of preparation for the greater anointing, the greater task and final destiny and purpose for his life that God had planned for him.

God is the greatest strategist and even in adversity God has His way. He works his purpose through your greatest and hardest of trials. Whatever the trial He is still God. He will do whatever He has to do to get you in your rightful place, especially when you fear Him and desire to be in the perfect will of God and not His 'permissive will'. In St. John 14:2-3 Jesus said, 'I go to *prepare a place* for you that where I am, there you may be also'. God can work his purpose out in your life even through affliction; there is nothing impossible for God. If we do not take heed to the call of God in our lives, know that hard times will come to us because God's will must and shall be done on the earth, as it is in heaven. Even Jesus learned obedience through the things that he suffered. Jonah obeyed God in the end, after he submitted to God in the belly of the fish.

Confusion may come, depression and discouragement may raise it's ugly head but God will come and pull you out of that mess, if you call on Him and wait on Him and allow the wind of the Spirit to blow and push you to that *specified place*.

It is important to obey the voice of the Holy Spirit as you receive instruction from Him, whether or not it makes sense to you. If it does not make sense to you it certainly will not make any sense to others. So as people begin to speculate, criticise and give their opinions, be true to God and hold on to what you know that you know, God spoke into your spirit and move out in obedience. Allow the will of God to be done in your life and for God to reign supreme and have authority over you.

Let God supply your **'BREAD'** according to His riches in glory!

> It is God that chooses our inheritance for us, the excellency of Jacob whom he loved.
>
> Psalms 47:4

God has gone ahead and chosen your inheritance for you. It is already settled in Heaven. Accept it, receive it and believe it and give God thanks for it in adavance!

**Fruitless Prayer**

For years after I separated from my children's father, I prayed for him to be saved. My children and I prayed and sometimes fasted together. We cried, bawled, fell down, hollered, jumped up, danced, spun around and did everything we possibly could for God to save him and return him to us, even though we hardly ever saw him.

I believed a lie which was that no man could ever love my children the way their biological father could, I mean really I don't know which planet my head was on! He was not playing an active role in their lives, but some how I convinced myself that one day he would come to his senses, stop listening to the negative words and influences of those around him and do what seemed to be the right thing. I believed that we would get married and live as a 'happy' family. The enemy Satan also sent his confirmations to reaffirm my belief. I told everyone just what I believed and when he married I still carried this strong belief. I thought that God would deliver him out of his religion and set him free. I also used the Word to back up my strong beliefs.

I found out much later on that I was in *denial* and being deceived by the spirit of *deception*. A part of my mind had been darkened resisting a true fact of life that had so evidently come but I refused to accept it. I loved the Lord and convinced myself that He would give me the desires of my heart because He said so in His word but I had misunderstood the scripture – Psalms 37:4-5. If you delight yourself in the Lord, He will give you the desire of your heart that *He, God placed there Himself*!

During this time God was using me to encourage people in the Lord and I have seen them grow strong in the Lord. I watched them get break-throughs and answers to prayers and I was left standing wandering, what's going on here Jesus? At this period in my life I spent hours on end in the presence of God just worshipping him, loving on him and reading my Bible, praying and just drawing close to God. But God uses the foolish things of this world to confound the wise – I Cor. 1:27. God is awesome you can not fathom Him out. Isaiah 55:8-9 – His ways are not our ways and His thoughts are not our thoughts. He is so much higher than us and His wisdom is past finding out!

**Honey from the Honeycomb**

For a duration of about six months when visiting the supermarket, I would suddenly start paying attention to the shelves filled with jars of honey. Also each time I opened up the cupboard in my kitchen where I kept the teabags, coffee and sugar I would literally see a jar of honey in the cupboard, that was not actually there. I would look at them in the supermarket read the labels and then place it back on the shelf. I kept thinking, I must buy some honey it's good for you and I used to drink it. I had no idea it was the Holy Spirit speaking to me expressly to buy the honey and begin to take it!

At this specific time I was well aware of the fact that on a regular basis I would wake up in the mornings and my eyes would have a stinging sensation and matter in it. When I began reading the Bible, tears would just start to flow from my eyes so much so that I could not read anything, everything became a blur! I was accustomed to reading my Bible for about three hours or more every morning first thing. I tried Optrex (eye cleanser) for a while but it proved to be expensive for me at that time as I was unemployed and always broke.

I realised this was no ordinary problem with my eyes but it was a spiritual attack from the devil. If I stayed up all night my eyes did not have that effect. I stayed up through the night sometimes because I just could not sleep at all. Before I committed my life to the Lord, when I couldn't sleep I would watch the television all night long whilst keeping busy with housework. Now I was saved and it was still happening so I decided to study my Bible and write down what the Holy Spirit would impart into my spirit, sing praises and pray all night long.

I finally obeyed the Holy Spirit and bought a jar of honey as the Holy Spirit had been leading and urging me to do. I would just use a spoonful of honey in my tea and coffee or take a spoonful of it and the problem with my eyes began to clear up. It was absolutely amazing! Then the Holy Spirit lead me to a passage of scripture in I Samuel 13:24-29.

*And the men of Israel were distressed that day: for Saul had adjured the people, saying, "cursed be the man that eateth any food until evening, that I may be avenged on mine enemies". So none of the people tasted any food.*

*And all they of the land came to a wood; and there was honey upon the ground. And when the people were come into the wood, behold, the honey dropped; but no man put his hand to his mouth: for the people feared the Oath.*

*But Johnathon heard not when his father charged the people with the Oath: wherefore he put forth the end of the rod that was in his hand, and dipped it in an* **honeycomb** *and put his hand to his mouth; and* **his eyes were enlightened**.

*Then answered one of the people, and said, "Thy father straitly charged the people with an Oath, saying, cursed be the man that eateth any food this day".* **And the people were faint.**

*Then said Johnathon, "My father hath troubled the land:* **see, I pray you, how mine eyes have been enlightened, because I <u>tasted</u> a little of this honey"**!

The honey had brought healing to my weak eyes. I now understand that God had given me the remedy to cure the problem with not only what was happening to my natural eyes but also my *spiritual eyes.* The thing that was causing me spiritual blindness and to be in denial in one particular area of my life was also affecting my life in the natural. I needed deliverance in my mind that's why Paul exhorts us to cast down imaginations and every high thing that exalts itself against the knowledge of God and bring every thought into captivity unto the obedience of Christ; II Cor. 10:5. It affected the way I saw this certain thing, and affected my perception of it and caused me to have certain negative dreams. It is important to know the source of your dreams. Not every dream you have comes from the Lord. It could be from the many thoughts going on in your head, or from the devil's agents. We must discern whether or not our dreams come from the Lord. Many times you will be able to line it up with the word of God and receive confirmation and a witness that it came from the Lord or ask the Lord is this dream from you particularly before we go running off to tell someone our dream. I know now there was a **stronghold** over a particular area of my mind that caused me to be in *denial* because of the traumatic break-up of my sinful relationship. The wages of sin is death and my life sure became hell on earth.

Some time after their father leaving I suffered a breakdown, after the ten-year relationship ended. I never sought any help for it, didn't realise I needed help and didn't know I had broken down because I just kept on going, doing what was right for the sake of the children like women do. I don't ever remember crying in the first few months and I later stopped speaking. I became extremely angry and bitter after some time. I had no outlet, and lost all our friends as a couple and all my personal friends and was left completely alone. I spent several hours per day just staring at the walls or the television. I spent long hours sleeping during the day whilst the children were at School to ease the pain. Three months after the break up I was made redundant which was a kind of blessing as I was able to fix up the house a little bit. Then life just became a living hell and continuous nightmare. I couldn't pay my bills, the mortgage, and the outstanding debts that I had been left alone to deal with. I wanted to sleep and never wake up. Even though I felt this way, I tried to go to Church when I could make the effort.

I visited my doctor once only, and he presented me with a prescription for some sleeping pills. I never went to the chemist to obtain them and never again returned to the doctor concerning my sleepless nights. My life just seemed to stop and stand still. I had never envisaged myself ever being in that position. But because of this I met my man JESUS.

Tasting the honey actually caused me to be able to spiritually see clearly my situation and condition and fully accept the **truth of the matter** and move forward in my mind.

When God brought me this understanding I had actually been saved for about four years and I remember one day feeling quite distressed about the situation, about my condition and my belief that God was going to save their father and turn everything around. I thought about all the mess and stuff, the horror of what I had been through and had been put through and I began to say Lord you mean you really want me to go back to all that mess I have left behind? To my great surprise and amazement He answered me and said, 'you are in denial'. I was in such a deep denial that I could not see properly and God used the honey as a medicine to deliver me and set me free and to affect my spiritual and physical vision making it much clearer. Ladies, men, please go out and buy yourselves a jar of honey if you are experiencing this type of denial and ensure that you always have one in the cupboard. Please don't continue to go through this kind of pain, *there is a balm in Gilead.*

I began to search myself and on that specific day and time I was preparing to attend a Prayer Summit at Elim Pentecostal Church. As I travelled on the bus I heard in my spirit, 'it's black and white'. Shortly after I arrived at the prayer conference, the speaker began to say, 'its black and white'. I can tell you that day, I allowed the Holy Spirit to get a hold of me, shake me up and deal with me firmly. God said the facts are black and white, like some things, they do not change, they are as you see them. Their father had by now converted to the Nation of Islam and settled down but I could not accept it because I was in denial. I thought that God loved me so much that anything I desired, I could have as long as I loved him back and obeyed His Word. After all, the

Bible says, commit your works unto the Lord and you know the rest. I believed I was doing everything the Lord wanted me to do at that time. I should be able to have what I desire? I was so wrong. Let my testimony deliver you please. We are here on this earth for Christ to live His life through us. Your life is not your own.

To reinforce what the Holy Spirit was revealing to me at this time, I also had a dream showing me that God had denied all my prayer requests on this subject. I thought of all the fasting and prayer my daughters and prayer partners had done over the years concerning this issue. In the dream, I went into a bank with their father to deposit a large amount of cheques but they all bounced and were returned to us when we returned. This was a confirmation that the Holy Spirit was now clearly telling me and I was able to accept it now properly, fully for the first time that he had rejected him from becoming my husband (thank you Jesus). Tears started to well up in my eyes as my deliverance came and I began to feel so relieved and silly at the same time. Then suddenly I stopped myself from spilling one tear.

If God was not going to give him to me then he must have someone else for me that someone is better than

I had expected or planned for myself. God makes the best choices for us. If he made me wait all this time, then he must have saved the best for last.

I heard the voice of the Holy Spirit say to me, "I took away a Saul to give you a David". Well now Saul represents stone, for he had a heart of stone, a very cold heart it was loveless, selfish and unkind. A heart filled with bitterness, anger, pride and jealousy! What did I expect he wasn't saved and real love comes from God because He is LOVE! God wanted me to have one of his kings, filled with the agape love of Jesus Christ. Wow!

It was then that I heard the Holy Spirit say, *"Leave the silver and choose gold"*. I pondered over it in my heart until about 2 weeks later, when I met up with an old family friend, someone who I had not seen for years, and had moved completely away from London. After speaking excitedly for about 2 or 3 minutes, she turned around and said to me as I walked away, 'Leave the silver and take the gold'. My mouth just fell open, and I was of course, speechless! God was speaking expressly to me again, for she had not known that God had said that very same word to me, this was another confirmation. I decided to go with her for *Sunday afternoon, lunch* and hear all about her new life as a Christian. At the end she handed me a book on marriage and it was amazing how we shared the same things and how God had dealt with her in a different way, but to bring out the same end. God used her to encourage me and just over a year later, she was married!.

I was so glad for the confirmation. I asked the Lord, since He knew that this man was not my husband all along, why didn't He tell me from the beginning? Why did he have to let me wait so long to tell me? Whilst thinking about the wasted time and energy I had put into all the hoping and the waiting, I became quite angry. All the prayers, all the fastings and all the encouragement and confirmation from other people also, telling me what I wanted to hear. All the time I had spent talking about it. The 'false hope' that I had thrived on and led my children to believe in the same way, with the same faith for their father to be saved and returned to us. My, my! What a waste! It had been a 'pipe dream'.

God answered me and said, 'I *allowed* you to believe it and do so in order for you to come after Me'. I almost felt as if I had been tricked, BUT I looked back again and remembered the times that I had spent in *prayer, fasting, praise and worship, thanksgiving*, spiritual warfare, because I was believing God for this man. The books I had read, the

Conferences I had attended. I had got prayer partners and prayer groups to pray for him and myself. God said because of my belief, I pursued God and my children also pursued God. We got close to Him, so close that we decided jointly, that whether or not God was going to bless us, we would just serve him anyway. You see God had to mature me before revealing it to me. I was not able to handle the rejection from those I loved and the pain of my past, it was too gross to even repeat, but God waited for the right moment before he set me free in this particular area of my life. Your salvation is truly over a period of time. It is a *process*. The negative things that had happened to me in my life had to be processed, whether I liked it or not, and in order for true inner healing and deliverance to take place.

Though I never became a nuisance to him, but the belief was a stronghold in my life. It was a strong imagination and delusion. The Bible says;

> *"Casting down imaginations and every high thing that exalteth itself against the knowledge of God and bringing into captivity every thought, to the obedience of Christ".*

II Corinthians 10:6

Yes, you can have a stronghold over your mind and be saved. You can believe a lie, you can be deceived by the devil and be saved. You can be overcome by evil because you opened your spirit to it. You made a choice not to trust in God and believe his Word and give Him the opportunity to do whatever He chooses to do with and in your life. You made up your own mind what you wanted. You chose fear over faith.

I chose to believe a *delusion* because all along God had been showing me that it wasn't him, but I did not understand what he was showing me. I could not interpret or understand my dreams. The spiritual people that I had around me and highly respected said they were too scared to reveal it to me, because of how it may have affected me, but there you go, I am alive and well, and grateful to God for not leaving me like that, but he went all the way for Me. He pulled me all the way up and all the way out, so that now I can breathe out and exhale my story, and face and walk in the truth.

There is a set time for God to reveal things to you, in order for you to understand where you came from, and why you had to go through some things that you went through.

Some of us ladies have dreams about a certain individual being our husbands. The men may be already engaged to someone else, but because of these dreams from the enemy of lust, we pursue these men and lust after them in our hearts. The devil is sowing these seeds of deception, false information or negative dreams into our minds, through a spirit of seduction and deception, and then we try to process them out! Please stop it now, for your own spiritual and physical, health and safety. Get angry and cast these dreams out of your mind and don't let the devil control the way you think, or live your life. Be free to serve the Lord totally in spirit and in truth.

I had no choice in the matter of writing this book. God told me to write it because there are so many women out there who are in the same predicament that I was in. So this book is for you my sisters in Christ Jesus. Please don't feel angry and put it down! God has so much he wants to share with you. He has your best interest at heart. He's your Father and wants so very much to give you good things, and to give you the best that He has but, we must come to him boldly through the blood of Jesus Christ the Son of God and we must come in spirit and in truth.

Release the old, in order to obtain the new. Enlarge your tent, lengthen your cords and strengthen your stakes (Isaiah 54:1-2). Expect to receive an abundance from the Lord, after you have sung a new song unto the Lord. If you are still waiting on God to bless you, sing. Sing until your increase comes. Sing until your money comes and until your debts have been cancelled through whatever channel God chooses to use. Sing until your husband comes, don't wait for him to come before you sing your song now. Angels can not sing your song for you, they have not been redeemed. No one else can sing your song for you because it's your testimony and so the angels will have to fold their wings as you sing unto the Lord. Others may have to listen to you as you sing your song because it will bring deliverance, when sung with understanding and maturity. Sing NOW!

**How do I get God's Desire?**

The desire of your heart is so important. As you get into the presence of the Lord and praise, worship, pray and read your bible, God will deposit his desires on the inside of your heart. God's Word must take up full residence and permanence in your heart. Let God rule and reign in your heart. When you do this, you will find that your prayers will change from *give me*, to **teach me**, show me, lead me, what, where, who, when. What is your way Lord of doing this? He will shew us, reveal to us the path of life, for in His presence there is fulness of joy, and at his right hand there are pleasures for evermore!

When God shows you His desire for your life, you must then in turn desire, what God has revealed to you in your spirit. Desire it with passion, with all your heart, what God has promised you. Therefore we are not following God for what we can get, but for who He is and the fact that we acknowledge his Lordship over our lives. Let our motives be based upon the agape LOVE of Jesus Christ and upon what God has said. At the end of the day your *relationship* between you and God is the most important thing! God will perform only what He has said. You need to study the Word of God.

God will not grant your request if it is not pleasing to Him, thank God. Father knows best and will take care of you! God made a 'better covenant' in order for you to have 'better things'. Our first and foremost lover is Christ and if God wishes to bless us with anything or anyone else, well it's His favour, good will and pleasure to do so, once you understand the purpose and reason for the blessing.

## CHAPTER 2

## ROMANCING THE KING

During our waiting time upon the Lord, He taught my daughters and I, in our praise and worship at home to dance in His presence. We would be singing love songs to the Lord, next thing we knew we would be on our feet dancing and waltzing with the Lord and each other. One two three, one, two, three, oh it was a delightful feeling. The joy that we would feel was so amazing. We would burst into fits of laughter for no apparent reason, but on the inside of our hearts God was dancing and waltzing and communing with us, whispering sweet nothings to us.

Solomon 1 verses 2-4

> *Let him kiss me with the kiss of his mouth: for thy love is better than wine.*

*Because of the savour of thy good ointments thy name is as ointment poured forth, therefore the virgins do love thee.*

*Draw me we will run after thee: the king hath brought me into his chambers: we will be glad and rejoice in thee, we will be glad and rejoice in thee, we will remember thy love more than wine: the upright love thee.*

I watched my children get up and dance gleefully and cheerfully in the presence of the Lord, run around the room, skip around in a circle and basically just have fun in the presence of God and it was wonderful. We had found real joy in the presence of the Lord and we discovered that truly the joy of the Lord is our strength. It wasn't just a scripture written on pages it had become real to us. The beauty of it is that we had been broken, depressed, sad, oppressed, and every kind of pressing because of the break up of the relationship that I had with their father and I did not know if we were ever going to really laugh and be happy again. This joy was new and we had never experienced anything like this before and so I grabbed a hold of it with both hands.

I would bring the songs to the prayer group at church and share it with my prayer partners and the same thing would happen. God would release an anointing of joy and we would get up and do the waltz and everyone would find a partner and we would dance before the Lord it was wonderful. We would laugh and get happy in God's presence it was such a delightful experience. We were all women whose spirits had been broken and crushed at some point in our lives and we were single parents, some divorced. All knowing and experiencing the hardship of growing up children without a father figure in our lives. We sang songs like, 'In moments like this, I sing out a love song to Jesus', 'My Jesus I love thee, I know thou art mine', and basically just romanced the Lord and made love to the Lord. It was like going on a secret rendezvous. The release of God's Joy in His presence was awesome. Even though each of us had equally enough problems to let any one stop trusting and believing in a God that is invisible and does things in His own time, you would never know it. Because in His presence there is fullness of Joy and at His right hand there are pleasures forever more (Psalms 16:11). Sometimes it was as if the Lord was tickling us and we would go into fits of laughter. Laughing and crying at the same time. The joy of the Lord was truly our strength.

## CHAPTER 3

## HEALING IN HIS PRESENCE

Exodus 15:26

*If thou wilt diligently hearken to the voice of the Lord thy God and wilt do that which is right in his sight, and wilt give ear to his commandments and keep all his statutes, I will put none of these diseases upon thee which I have brought upon the Egyptians:* **for I am the LORD that healeth thee.**

*I discovered that Worship is a medicine. It's soothing and healing.*

Solomon 1:3

*'Because of the savour of thy good ointments, His name is as ointment poured forth, therefore do the virgins love thee'.*

Pain, pushed me into the presence of God. Whenever things would go wrong, I would run into the presence of the Lord, sometimes screaming, shouting, angry, kicking, sometimes just silent and numb. I remember one day the bailiff came to the house and somehow I managed by the grace of God, to get rid of him without a struggle or fight. He in fact, was quite okay. But after I closed the door, I felt so embarrassed and so ashamed that I ran into my living room, into a corner and sat down and cried, hugging my knees and feeling absolutely helpless. But I heard the Lord say, 'all my springs are within you', Psalms 87;7 which meant that I had the power of God in me, to teach me how to get out of this mess. I needed to tap into God's method of bringing me out of this financial disaster. Everything I needed was in me. Initially I thought the debt would just disappear one day but he kept on returning and so I had to begin to pay the outstanding debt!

Because I would constantly worship the Lord, He gave me the strength and grace to cope with the situation and after I worshiped, things didn't seem that bad anymore.

The intensity of the pain goes away even though the situation still exists.

During some real struggles I really acted like a little child, and would just stretch my arms up to God and say help me. I tried to get others to be a part of my pity party but God would speak through the children and say 'just praise Me'. My daughter would come into the bedroom and say Mum, the Lord said read Psalms 149 which says 'Let the high praises of God be in their mouth, and a two-edged sword in their hand'. Your victory is in your praise. The Lord used them to encourage me. The Word was in them.

Worship is like taking a pain-killer for a headache or toothache, the severity and intensity of the pain goes away even though the problem is still there and the tooth needs to be extracted, you get a certain amount of relief from the pain. So in worship my fears and anxieties were calmed and subsided and the peace of God would come upon me and within me and around me. I felt like a new person. The enemy would be silenced and flee.

The children were a tower of strength at times like these. Somehow, God just kept them strong for me. They would encourage me and there was a lot of love.

We were in unity, and there is strength in unity and in unity there dwells the blessing. As young as they were, God used them to bless me with words of encouragement.

I believe that because of the daily prayers and worship times that we spent before the Lord, God just dealt with all of the debris, and took care of us in every way. God did not allow the enemy to have the victory over us. Many times the devil tried to sow seeds of hatred and resentment and unforgiveness. But I had to keep on confessing aloud, I choose to forgive and call their names and say God bless them and keep them and cause your face to shine upon them and lift up your countenance upon them and give them peace (Numbers 6:25-26). Heal them and heal me Lord.

Even when we become mature in Christ, He still wants us to run into Him with every problem, every need, and seek His face and fellowship with Him and rely and depend upon Him. You will never be all sufficient and independent of God. You will continue to need Him every step of the way. The day you think you can get along without God will be the day of your destruction. Man needs God like flowers need rain, like fish need water to live in, like the earth needs the sun to shine in the day and the moon to shine at night. Creation needs God, we too need God.

As we sent up our prayers and our worship to the Lord, He gave us constant healing and deliverances and we were able to get up and continue in the race. There was also a time when I suffered terribly with migraine, to the point where I could not even lift my head off the pillow and sometimes vomiting. But one night in church as my head was pounding away, I decided to go home because of the pain. As the Pastor was preaching, he paused to allow a few people to get up and say, I slipped and I fell, and I'm back, at which point after standing and confessing this, I felt the power of God hit me. The yoke was destroyed and I was set free and to this day I have not suffered in that way again. Obviously, the devil has tried to bring it back but I would just rebuke it and remind the devil that God healed me from this thing.

One night the devil came into my bedroom and whispered in my ear, if you stop praising God I'll leave you alone. Even though I was fast asleep the Holy Spirit kicked in and I raised my hands in the air and shouted 'The Lord is my Shepherd I shall not want'. Immediately, the devil had to flee from me. Your praises are effective.

Never stop praising God, whether you understand what is going on in your life or not. He is worthy of your praises, the devil uses your problems to distract you but praise God and stay focused and you will have the victory!

Psalms 42

> As the hart panteth after the water brook, so my soul panteth after thee O God. My soul thirsteth for God, for the living God.

A hart when chased by its attacker or hunter runs to find water, a river because when it runs into the water the enemy loses its scent, and cannot continue the chase any longer. So it is with the devil. If you run into the presence of the Lord with your praises, whilst you are being hunted, provoked, and distracted or afflicted by the enemy, begin to worship God and pray to your God and he will back off. He will lose your trail or scent because you found your refuge in the secret place of the most high, the presence of God. The devil cannot stand praise and worship and if he tries to disrupt the praises then use the word of God to throw him off. The Word of the Lord shall prevail, apply the blood of Jesus and remind the devil of his defeat by Jesus.

## RADICAL PRAISE

The Lord also taught me to praise Him in a radical way. I remember that almost every Saturday morning I would be ill. A certain individual would visit the house and after leaving I would go into fits of sneezing and coughing and my eyes would be streaming with tears and have a tingling sensation. Even when the individual stopped coming it still happened. It became like a routine. Then one day God showed me the source, human spirits would come into the house up to my bedroom in the morning and release something into the atmosphere and this would start the attack. This would also happen to me on a bus, if anyone came on who was very heavily oppressed or say a tramp, immediately I would start to sneeze and cough and my eyes would tingle and start to run gallons of water. I realised there must be an open door in my life and I needed desperately to be healed.

One particular Saturday I had enough and after praying the Lord gave us an invitation to praise him. He spoke to us through Psalms 117:

*O praise the Lord all ye nations: praise him all ye people. For his merciful kindness is great toward us*

*and the truth of the Lord endureth for ever. Praise
ye the LORD.*

We praised God in every room of the house, we jumped
and danced and ran and did everything we knew to
do. We read the Psalms aloud and sang and shouted
as loud as we could. This went on for about an hour
and a half or two, and then we ended up with a type of
Indian style dance, laughing and falling on the floor. At
the end I noticed I was not coughing or sneezing any
more and I felt as fit as a fiddle. I couldn't believe it. I
put my trainers on and we walked all the way to our
local store. Praise God that after a period of time this
completely stopped. Our warfare was accomplished.
Your VICTORY is truly in your PRAISE!

# CHAPTER 4

## HEALING IS A PROCESS

Isaiah 1:6

> *From the sole of the foot even unto the head there is no soundness in it: but wounds and bruises and putrifying sores: they have not been closed, neither bound up, neither mollified with ointment.*

Even though I was now saved, I was still in a lot of internal pain. I was getting ahead vibrantly in my spiritual life but every so often a particular issue would arise. It would come on suddenly. I experienced this terrible pain in my stomach for about five years or so. It can happen at any time of the day or night. A sudden intense pain would hit me just under my navel and at times I would see a small lump pushing out. I would feel the need to rush to the bathroom and empty my bowels. Whilst actually passing stools I would get extremely hot to the point where I had to strip off every piece of my clothing. As soon as I finished my temperature would drop, but the pain in my stomach would increase, and sometimes I literally crawled back to my bedroom and spent the next few days in bed. Sometimes I would bleed profusely but it wasn't like a period. Breathing became difficult but thank God for some strong prayer partners who would pray for me throughout this time. I would cry out to God and then someone would phone. But at the end of the day nobody could help me I still needed the touch of God's hand.

When I asked God what this was all about He just said, 'further along you'll know all about it'. God will not tell you everything about everything and He doesn't have to He's God. Some things God waits until we are spiritually mature and emotionally stable before He reveals it to us. God did not reveal to Jacob that Joseph was alive during all the years he mourned and grieved for him, believing he was actually dead. Until the right season and appointed time during that season. Our time isn't God's time, but God's time is when you are ready and the time is ripe for all things to be revealed in the open. Understanding comes for the things that God has prepared for you, and your times and seasons are in His hands.

My fear of really knowing what was making me ill was so great, that I refused to go to the doctor. Ignorance, in my book at that time was bliss. I began to cry out to the Lord for healing and deliverance. I feared having surgery and for as long as I could help it nobody was going to cut me open for no reason.

I went to Morris Cerullo, Mission to London meetings and Benny Hinn, and I saw people walk out of their wheel chairs, the lame walk the blind see, deaf ears hear and still I did not receive my healing.

The Word that the Lord kept on giving me was Exodus 15:21.

> *"I am the God that healeth thee from all your diseases".*

God instructed Moses to make a fiery brass serpent and set it on a pole and told him to hold it up to the people and lift it up in the wilderness. He said, as long as they looked on the Golden Serpent they would be healed. But those who did not look on it for healing died (Numbers 21:8).

This Golden Serpent represented a future figure of Christ, when he became a curse for his people and hung on a cross. He died so that we may live. When you have been stung by lifes' bitter cup, you need healing whether you recognise it or not. Keep your eyes and focus on Jesus. He will heal you.

One day I was driving home after taking the children to school and the Lord dropped a Word in my spirit. I pulled the car over and took out my Bible and read Isaiah 1:6, and the Holy Spirit said to me 'healing is a process'. I felt discouraged and distraught that my healing was not going to be immediate as my emotions were a mess. Even so many times I went into fasting and prayer and crying and screaming, hoping God would speed up the timing and process, but it was not so. God has a specific timing for your healing and it is also connected to your obedience. One of the first things I learned was that I was going to have to make peace, in some instances with the same people that I had no desire to see or hear from whilst I was in this condition. Some of those people had hurt my children and myself. They had rejected us and it was not an easy thing to live with. When my prayer partner first told me to pray for them I said you must be insane. To think that God would want to save their lives, they are too wicked. But I really did not understand the love of Christ. Eventually after a real struggle of even mentioning their name in prayer, their names would falter and stammer on my lips. The children would pray for them easily but I really struggled. It got easier and easier. When God did actually begin to save them I could not believe it, even though we prayed for them to be saved. I saw them in Church lifting up hands worshiping God and now I had no choice but to make peace as God had instructed me in my dreams.

The wounds were very deep so the bitterness and unforgiveness was very deep. Even though I was trying hard to forgive the devil kept trying to keep me walking in unforgiveness. Even when I did forgive them it still hurt for a very long time it was really painful, and I wondered would I ever get past the pain and could I ever be made whole again? The devil would keep on rehearsing the whole event over and over again in my ear. But I kept on saying aloud bless them Jesus, from the crown of their head to the soul of their feet.

I sent them love and peace and joy. Do a new thing in them Jesus. I had to make confessions with my mouth to free myself and them from any resentment and hatred that was trying to take root in my heart. We must keep our heart with all diligence, for 'out of the abundance of the heart the mouth speaks' and your heart belongs to God. We must ask him and invite him to rule and reign supreme in every room in our hearts and not just in one part, He wants all of our heart.

Even so I thought, I've forgiven them but I don't have to speak to them or have anything to do with them. But that's where the real test of forgiveness comes in. If they tried to make contact I ran the other way as fast as I could. I did not trust them and I didn't want them around me, neither did I want to face them because there was a lot of shame there. I hid from everyone and everything that represented my past. I nursed my shame, walked around my shame and my shame became an idol before God. I wouldn't let anyone near me seeing as sooner or later I felt they would let me down or hurt me. Certain places I refused to go and instead of shopping at my local shopping centre I drove further away so I did not have to bump into any one. I ducked and dived and the shame of my past became a stronghold in my life. Fear would grip me in the nights and I had countless sleepless nights. My home was plagued with fear. The Bible says that 'perfect love casteth out all fear', but I did not understand God's perfect love.

In the daytime whilst in the presence of the Lord, everything was fine but the nights became a nightmare and I hated the night. I couldn't sleep very well so I studied the Word of God, praised and worshiped Him. I would have midnight rendezvous with the Lord. That was like having a midnight lover. It was wonderful! There were also times of prayer and intercession. After a few hours sleep I would wake up and pray again before daylight. God would just strengthen me and refresh me so I never really felt tired, and I did not have to catch up on any sleep in the daytime. Maybe sometimes only after spiritual warfare in the prayer room, as it made me physically tired.

I realised after a long period of time that even though I needed to be healed I was afraid to be healed. One day the pain in my stomach was so excruciating that I called a friend and she advised me to call the doctor. I did, but he refused to come out and see me. He said that if you are still the same in two hours call me back. The pain subsided and I decided not to go. Previously the Lord had given me a new song to sing:

> I am the Lord that healeth thee,
>
> Lift up your head, don't be afraid,

For I am the Lord that healeth thee.

These words came in my spirit and suddenly the pain started again so I called the doctor again and he told me to come. He gave me such an examination that by the time he finished I was in more pain. I spent the next day or two in bed. On the Sunday morning KICC began a week of meetings, 'The Gathering of Champions' and I was determined to go, live or die. Morris Cerullo would be there and perhaps I would get my healing at last. Brother Cerullo announced that people would be healed all the way to the back of the Church, which was at the time about 4,500 people. I said yes, I'm in the right place, but it did not happen that day.

On Thursday of that week, Bishop Morton was preaching on knowing your enemy. During the altar call his wife took the microphone and began to sing these words:

'I am the Lord that healeth thee,

I am the Lord your healer.

I sent my word and healed your disease,

I am the Lord your healer'.

I had sung that particular song so many times and right away I lifted up my hands toward heaven and began to cry out in my seat, to Jesus. I begged him please, please, don't pass me by. I cried and cried and hollered and then I felt the presence of the Lord as if hovering over me. I felt a heat come upon me and I began to rejoice and cry and laugh all at the same time and give thanks. I almost had to be carried out the building, I could hardly stand for laughing.

The joy I felt that night is indescribable. I was the driver and only the Holy Spirit led me home that night because we laughed all the way home. Since that day I have been completely healed in that area. A couple of times afterwards the enemy has tried to bring it back but I reminded him that I was healed at the Gathering of Champions at KICC and I don't accept anything that he brings any more, for I am a child of God. I declared the word of God.

Isaiah 53:5

> 'He was wounded for my transgressions and He was bruised for my iniquities, the chastisement of my peace was upon Him and by His stripes we are healed'.

Months later I went to the hospital for an examination. The doctor said there is nothing wrong with you, you are a healthy young woman, praise the name of the Lord and give thanks unto him for his mercies endureth forever.

God was cleaning me up and purging me of all the bitterness and the gall, the sorrow and fear and anger. All these things had to be purged and burned out of me. God was burning up the sin and dross in me in order for me to be made whole. These are the things that give an open door to the enemy to come and afflict you because of all the unforgiveness and bitterness in your heart and the pain of your past that you refuse to let go of, denying the power of the cross to be effective in your life. You feel this way because of the unresolved issues in your life.

Release everything and everyone to God, these things hinder you from being blessed of God from receiving your inheritance. His yoke is easy and His burden is light. Cast your cares upon Jesus for he cares for you. It's not worth your life, your sanity, your future and your children's future holding onto all of the hurt and the pain of your past.

For the healing to take place you must be processed through fiery trials. Also, the Lord will instruct you to do something that may seem very simple and because of the hurt you find it hard to do. If you obey, it will bring about your healing for healing is a process it does not always just come like that.

There are some things in us that will only come out when we go through the fire. The fire won't burn you but it takes out of you the things that are not bringing glory to God. If you are going to carry the glory of God in your earthen vessel and it be revealed in your life, then the 'process' is very necessary in every area of your life.

The refiners fire and fullers soap is vital, essential and most important for purging, cleansing and washing. When you come out God takes away the sting, the pain of the memory of your past, in order for you to go forward in to your destiny.

In Genesis 41;51, Joseph has his first son and calls him Manasseh and said, 'for God hath made me forget all my toil and all my father's house'. God will give you something to make you forget the pain of your past and the struggles that you had. It may be a testimony that you will be able to carry wherever you go. In some cases God will give you something tangible to make a difference in your life. God gave Ruth a husband, Boaz who was extremely wealthy and gave her a son whom they named Obed. He was the father of Jesse and Jesse was the father of David. For Naomi who lost her husband and two sons, God gave her Ruth, Boaz and a grandson, she nursed him as her own. There is hope in our end. It is God's will to do us good in our latter end (Jeremiah 29:11) God promised to restore health to us and heal our wounds and to glorify His name through us and in us so that we will offer up true sacrifices of praises and 'thanksgiving' from the heart.

Looking back I can agree that it was good for me that I was afflicted, because it drove me to seek the Lord, to worship Him and Him alone. It taught me how to love him. I am head over heals in love with Jesus Christ, what a Man! What Christ can do for you no other human being on the face of the planet earth can do for you. *You need Christ* in your life every day to make your life complete and worth living. Everything else you receive is just a bonus, from the mercy and favour of God.

I remember the times when I had no money and I was totally dependent upon the finance that my children's dad would provide for them on a weekly basis. Well he came when it was convenient for him to do so. But then the Lord would call us into a time of praise and worship and give us the specific songs to sing so as to bring about deliverance, for God does send us songs of deliverance like he did for King David. Shortly afterwards, God would make him show up, I did not have to call him and ask him what's happened, or where are you, all I had to do was sing the songs of Zion. Your victory is in your praise. Sometimes I could not sing but I would hear my spirit singing and the same results were obtained. God is so good. He would also sometimes speak in our time of praising Him, but one thing I know He never left us alone or without. He never let us down.

During the first couple of years of separating, my children's dad became a muslim in the Nation of Islam. Unsuccessfully, he tried to convert me into this religion but the Holy Spirit lifted up a standard against the enemy's plans, which came to nought. To me it was more profitable to serve the true and living God regardless of what I had and did not have. I could not possibly believe that a religion founded in the 7th Century based on one man's experience with a fallen angel could be true. Where was God before the 7th Century? I would rather have no other religion than set up or believe in a false god and call him my god and bow down to it. It just didn't make sense to me. When you know the truth it makes you free and keeps you free. I chose LIFE.

Soon afterwards he changed his name and got married. But I believed in my heart and with all my heart that God was still going to save him and put us back together so that we could be a family again. I received words of confirmation also that this would take place. I know now that the devil will send people your way to confirm his lies to you. Remember he's a counterfeit, so he tries to do everything that God does, he'll send people to prophesy lies to you in order to keep you believing a lie. This became a stronghold in my life and only God could and would deliver me in His time.

I told just about everyone that God was going to save him, so when the marriage went ahead you can just imagine the embarrassment I felt. I saw myself in a dream being carried through the streets, nailed to a cross and the streets were crowded with people, they were all laughing and mocking and jeering at me. Oh the shame I felt. I continued to hide away from people and once again, turned my face and whole heart towards God. I'll live. I choose to live.

## SOUL TIE

God wants all of your heart and soul but the trouble
is we seem to reserve just one room in our hearts for
ourselves, for our own desires, will and delights. As we
desire these men in our past for ourselves, we blot out
what God has for us. We must break the soul ties of
past relationships in our lives that hinder us from getting
closer to God, and moving forward in our lives to bring
healing and deliverance. We must close the chapters in
our lives, turn over a new page and allow God to do a
new thing in us and for us. Let us hope, trust and have
confidence in the Word of God. Give God room to
work. Let go of the past and embrace the future, God is
waiting for you. Your future is waiting on you!

# CHAPTER 5

## ALL THAT GLITTERS IS NOT 'GOLD'

Deception is on the increase in these last days and Satan is sending out counterfeits to Gods' people, making it look and sound like the real thing to make you miss out on what God really has for you. For example, that woman or man who presents them selves constantly in your face and covers you with hugs and kisses, and embraces you at every opportunity making you feel so wanted and desirable, we must discern what is of God and what is not, otherwise we will end up with the wrong partners, we will end up with Ishmael and not Isaac. It is said, that just when God is about to bless you that the enemy will always try to send you a counterfeit and if you are not careful, you will believe a lie and go ahead with your own decisions, thinking this is the one

I have been praying to God for. The devil is a liar and deceiver and is very professional at what he does.

The wheat and the tares grow together and look alike, but the tares are very hurtful, harmful and bring confusion and pain. We must learn to discern specifically what is real and what is false. We can only do this if our hearts are pure if our hearts are full of the spirit of truth, and love the truth and the Word of God is embedded deeply into our hearts.

The devil brings us dreams in the night. As we sleep the enemy sets to work. He'll bring you fake dreams showing you that this man is my husband because the man came up to you in the dream and kissed you. But so did Judas kiss Jesus at the instant of betrayal, when he had brought the soldiers to arrest him. The enemy hides his true thoughts behind a kiss and will be there every time you feel down. The enemy makes you feel down and then gets him to phone you and you think that it's the Holy Spirit drawing you closer together, when all along it was the evil plot of the devil, or the lusts of your flesh.

Sometimes we are just vulnerable and we open up ourselves to the devil (not intentionally) giving him access. We must allow the Spirit of God to draw us into His presence and not be led by our flesh.

We as women, are so desperate to be fulfilled in a relationship that we are easily seduced by the spirit of lust among us, that instead of resisting it when it comes, we embrace it, because it makes you feel good. In doing so we open ourselves to being seduced and then deceived. We must not continue in this sin, we must be free, we must break free from these lusts of the flesh and bring our bodies under subjection to the Holy Spirit because our bodies are the temple of the living God and He is Holy and requires us to be Holy and pure in our hearts.

Your counterfeit will call you late at night instead of at a convenient, decent hour, and is only available at inconvenient times. He counsels secretly, maps his steps carefully and weighs his words before speaking.

The real thing is just around the corner. God will tell you to 'stay close' to Him, but we have been distracted and don't really hear God. When you don't stay close to God, you set yourself up to go through traumatic experiences. Events come and take you by surprise. Devastation is inevitable, pain and confusion is inevitable, because you forgot what God told you. It may be that you got caught up in the moment of things and instead of standing back, looking from a distance. We wonder, 'how did I get here'? The wedding is announced and you are not the bride. Hasten to the Father, run to Him and worship with all your heart.

# CHAPTER 6

## RUTH & BOAZ

Naomi a widow, had returned to Bethlehem after leaving for ten years with her husband and two sons. Naomi returned only with one of her daughter-in-laws, RUTH. Naomi returned in distress, empty handed, bitter and angry (Ruth 1:20). God had not dealt with her in the way that she would have liked so she said call me Marah instead, which means bitter. Naomi's husband and two sons had passed away.

At the set time when they returned, it was the beginning of the barley harvest season. In Ecclesiastics 3, God is a God of perfect timing. This was the perfect timing of God, the set time to favour Naomi and Ruth in their brokenness, barrenness and bitterness. She was at her lowest state, ripe for God to bring change to her already desperate situation, and to show off his glory to them.

Naomi instructs Ruth to 'wash herself' clean up and make herself look good and attractive, smell good. Put on her best clothes and lay her head on Boaz's feet in the night in the threshing floor. Lift up his skirt and put her head on his feet.

- Wash off your past, smell, scent, malice, pride arrogance, bitterness, resentment, negative views.

- Put on humility, gentleness, meekness, kindness, purity, love.

- People have been hurt but it is time to be healed.

As a woman laying her head at his feet she was making a statement to Boaz, in a humble and right way. This was their custom at that time. Let me explain.

If your husband dies and you own land and property that you can not maintain, to keep it in the family, you are supposed to sell the land and the house to the next male family member in line, so as to keep it in the family as a heritage. So Boaz was a type of Christ in the sense that he would REDEEM the land from his other family member. With it came Naomi and Ruth a 'responsibility' and 'liability' because it would cost him to take care of the older woman, Naomi.

Widows in Jew or Greek society were known as dumb, they were not valid or valued. They had no say in matters, and were vulnerable. They were poor but Boaz 'Redeemed' them from the poverty and shame that they had suffered in the past. They received double for their shame. (ISAIAH 54) They received a Jubilee Blessing in the year of Jubilee/Release/Redemption. Their inheritance was saved by the fact that Naomi knew the law. 'Ignorance' does not pay. God will not bless ignorance. You have to find things out. Look for information from God seek him, discover his word and present his word to him with understanding and knowledge to move forward in your life.

The man or woman God has for you may need to be ministered to. The have gone through pain and suffering and abuse, broken lives and relationships. They need to be cared for. They may be sensitive and fragile, and one will be stronger than the other at first. Both will compliment each other, as God will make everything beautiful in his time.

The other next of kin was approached by Boaz but he only wanted the house, land and material things, not the responsibility of Ruth a moabitess, poor and of no quality class, no calibre, not fit for his family name. Nor an old woman to be a noose around his neck that would be too embarrassing and shameful for him. So he passed the buck and shifted the responsibility to Boaz.

This man was not spiritually mature enough to accept this, unwilling and had no heart of compassion. Just greed. He probably did not know the true love of a father, therefore could not act like one. God would have shown him what to do and how to act. He missed out on a chance to bring in the greatest Psalmist that ever lived; David, the Servant of God.

Boaz was a Redeemer and 'father figure' with a heart of love, compassion and humility. He showed the love of our Father which is in Heaven. He loves and cares for the poor and needy, the down and outs, the outcasts of society. He was willing to share of his wealth with them and to give himself to them, regardless of the criticisms and reaction, comments and negative remarks of the people. He displayed the love of Jesus Christ, and recognized Ruth as a virtuous woman.

## FINISH IT!

As previously stated, Boaz reflects Christ. He represents Christ the Redeemer, the Saviour and Intercessor. The other man whose right it was to redeem, though like every other man found her attractive but had no honourable intentions towards her. Though he agreed to redeem Ruth from her past and present condition, he was not interested in also taking on board her mother-in-law, she was a burden. This man had not the love of Christ in him and could not show her due respect because he was not meant to be her Redeemer, even though he was next in line.

We know that Ruth was a beautiful woman because she had a virtuous and humble spirit, and is described as a virtuous woman. She had an inner beauty that shone on the outside of her. Everyone observed that she had been faithful, loyal, honourable and respectful to Naomi, this is what makes her a virtuous woman.

When Ruth approached Boaz she discovered that there was a 'hitch' and he then set about dealing with the matter, Naomi says to Ruth 'he will not rest until he has finished the thing this day'. She was also told to 'sit still' until you know how the matter will fall, and it was her faith and wisdom to 'sit still'. Stand still and see the salvation of the Lord, see how God would work things out. See how God would deliver her in this situation. Ruth could not do any more than wait in 'anticipation' and 'expectancy' of what God was about to do. She waited with faith in the God of Naomi. Ruth had to focus on God whilst she kept herself still, her hope and confidence was in God and in him alone. She hoped to be shown favour from the Lord and did not try to work out the answer for herself. She lifted her eyes unto the hills from whence cometh her help. Her help cometh from the Lord which made heaven and earth (Psalms 121). We must wait for the answer with praise and thanksgiving, because if God said it then it is already done!

Ruth was well aware of the fact that Boaz, a kinsman was a respectful and honourable man. A man of honour, well known, highly esteemed and of good character. Boaz was determined to finish what had been started. Christ will not leave us alone until he has done that thing which he promised to do for us. He will not rest, he never slumbers or sleeps, and He is busy working things out for us. He will not leave us comfortless.

Boaz blessed Ruth by giving her six measures of barley for her mother-in-law; this shows his concern and care, the love of Christ, concern for her welfare as well as Ruth's. He was already providing and making a way for her. He had enough love and care, and compassion for both of them. He displayed the love of the Lord Jesus Christ. The other kinsman's concern was limited to Ruth and no further, he did not want the burden of an old woman around him. There was no compassion in him, no real love!

Leave the Silver and choose Gold!

Boaz was well known and made great because of what he did for Ruth and Naomi. He was lead by God and helped to take their shame and reproach away. He redeemed them from their past, he was honourable and respectful, he had the heart of the Father, God, a heart of compassion and true Christ like love.

**Obedience!**

In all of this Ruth was completely obedient. She followed the instructions given to her by Naomi, who told her to wash and dress and uncover and lay her head on Boaz feet. She was instructed to wait until he had finished eating and drinking. She followed the instructions completely. When our obedience is fulfilled then, we can expect to see the blessing come into manifestation. Obedience is the KEY!

In St. John Chapter 2, the servants are instructed by Jesus' Mother, Mary to obey whatever Jesus said. They had to carry the earthen pots to the well to fill it with water, so it took a while. But they obeyed the illogical instruction, and as they did so and 'poured out' the water into the glasses it became wine. It was indeed a miracle! *LOOK for a MIRACLE. EXPECT a MIRACLE in the name of JESUS!*

You must go all the way to receive your miracle, half way won't do. It may be painful, right now but push and continue. It may become hard, you may start to think I can't do this it's too hard. But speak to your mind and soul and spirit and command it to move in accordance with GOD's Word and Spirit. Synchronise your spirit to move at the same time as God's Spirit. Be in tune to the Holy Spirit and receive from the Lord. He is going out of His way to come to you and bless you. Be careful that you are the cause of your own hold up. The last mile is the absolute hardest. On this journey to the end, everything in you will resist the Spirit of God. You feel drained. You have just about enough strength to get up in the morning but push with all your might. Praise like you never praised before, then do whatever God tells you to do.

The promise must be birthed through your flesh. The spirit and the flesh war against each other. When you go to do good, evil presents itself. You must persevere and persist at this point, you can make it to the end. In the end, God's word will come to pass.

One Sunday after Service, a young respectable brother said to me, 'your husband is coming'. Who is he, I thought? Should I go seeking him? Is he lost in the first place? No. Is it the nearest brother to you who is paying special attention to you, but not quite saying what his real intentions are! Does he evade certain personal questions when put forward to him? Yet, when you're around him you feel like a strong powerful magnetic pulling force that's drawing you to him and it seems like hey, this could be the one. It's so deceptive, but so appealing is the spirit of LUST. Yes I said lust! So inviting yet so cunning. So tasty and yet so harmful. So demanding and yet so seemingly innocent. So delightful but yet so sly. So like the one that the Lord has promised me but the motive is LUST not love, the counterfeit and not the real thing. Yet I must seek God for His Counsel and Wisdom, for truly and indeed as the scripture says, 'Eyes have not seen and ears have not heard, neither has it entered into the hearts of men, the things that God has prepared for those that love Him. (I Cor.2:9) God will reveal to us by His Spirit what He has for us individually and personally.

From then on I heard what I wanted to hear, and did not hear, what I did not want to hear. Again things were having a form of godliness but I was denying the power of God moving in my life. Resisting the will of God coming in my life, and imagining my life just the way I wanted it. The Bible says 'Cast down every imagination and every high thing that exalts itself above the knowledge of God and bringing every thought into captivity and unto the obedience of Christ (II Cor. 10:5).

**Cupboard Love**

This term means the wrong motives behind the relationship you are involved in. Sure enough, if God did not say it, it will not come to pass, even though you are praying without cease, and sealing everything with the blood of Jesus.

The Holy Spirit told me that He would expose the 'Cupboard Love'.

Through the spirit of lust, many marriages have come together and this is the wrong motive. Whether it just be the need to be married or lust for the financial security, the comfort of marriage', or just so you don't end up alone, people or women accept what seems to be available at the time with no consultation from God. Consulting only with 'friends'. People have also married because someone told them who their 'chosen' partner is, and did not seek the Lord for themselves. Later they said, 'I don't think this is the right one after all', when it's too late and after they have already said, 'I do'.

**Spiritual Rape**

The spirit of lust seduces you and then rapes you and has its wicked way with you, with your consent, because you allowed yourself to entertain it at some stage. Lust just needs an open door to come through. It will wake you up in the night time in your bedroom. It will visit you and rape you. It will come and you may never know until it's just about ready to leave, or you wake up and feel pain in your body in certain areas. You wake up in certain positions and so on. This results in a spiritual bondage/tie. But by the power of the blood of Jesus Christ, I break that lusting spirit right now. I destroy it with the consuming fire of the Lord. I close the door on it and I say get out in the name of Jesus you are trespassing on God's property, I don't belong to you. I am a child of God and I belong to the King of kings and the Lord of lords. I release the blood all around you.

This can also affect your monthly menstruation, and affects various parts of the female organs (eg. fibroids). Causing irregular periods, or no periods.

It's time for us to shut the door in the spirit realm on the demonic activities. We are to resist the devil and he will flee from us. We must rebuke the devil off of our minds. Every time he comes with the thoughts that seem to be pleasing to the flesh we must exercise the weapons of our warfare, which are not carnal but mighty through God to the pulling down of strongholds. Give the enemy no entrance. Close every door to him. Fight with all your might. Your body is the temple of the living God, the Holy Ghost. It's time for us to stop defiling the temple of God. It's time to prepare ourselves to be a sanctuary, so that God can dwell in us as clean vessels of the Lord. We must present our bodies to God as a living sacrifice pure and holy.

**Prayer:-**

Father, in the name of Jesus prepare us to be a sanctuary for you, and forgive us for defiling your temple. Help us to turn from our own desires and deposit your desires in us. Wash us Lord and cleanse us from all uncleanness and lusts of the flesh and break every yoke of bondage in our lives Lord. Lead us in the way everlasting and into your truth, in the name of Jesus Christ. Amen.

We must allow God to do a new thing in us, He is the Potter we are the clay, when He is finished moulding and shaping us and fashioning us after himself then we will be able to walk in victory.

Your health is at stake, your spiritual health is at risk. Your spiritual development will be deficient and impeded and hindered. Think about how much time you spend entertaining the thoughts of the things and person that you are allowing yourself to lust after or is lusting after you. Change your thought pattern. Whatsoever things are pure, whatsoever things are lovely, think on these things (Philippians 4:8). It will be healthier for you and more rewarding for your spiritual inner man. Be not deceived, God is not mocked, if you sow to the flesh you will reap to the flesh, which is corruption.

When Eve was in the Garden of Eden, she spent a great deal of time looking at the tree that she was forbidden to eat from. The more she looked at the forbidden fruit is the more she desired it, and the more she desired it the more she was lured to it. The more enticing it became. The evil serpent drew her to it by his deceptive magnetic forcible power and she resisted it only for a time. As he persisted in drawing her to it, finally after entertaining the thoughts of the devil, 'hath God said, what did God say'? Are you sure? This caused her to contemplate what God had originally said to her and contemplation is sin. May be he meant it this way or may be he meant it that way. Eve entered a two-way conversation with the devil, because she contemplated what God said. Contemplation is a spirit. She discussed what God said with the devil, rather than going back to the Word or her husband for the final deciding factor, or to God for a reminder of what he previously said in His instructions. Disobedience was the result.

I distinctively remember that when I asked the Lord what he was showing me concerning a certain matter God said, I'm showing you what is in his heart. I shared it with others and they said that's your husband. Then I decided to believe what they said, as every one said it had been confirmed to them. God's voice and word over-powers everyone else's and cancels out the comments and opinions of others. I was young in the Lord but I would follow on to know Him.

The devil opposed what God said and told Eve a lie, which she believed. 'You shall not surely die' Eve and Adam both died a spiritual death, when their naked human eyes were opened. Confusion set in spiritual blindness set in, now they could only see through the eyes of carnality and what they saw was themselves, they experienced for the first time, shame, embarrassment, corruption and exposure and for the first time they knew they were naked. They hid themselves from God, in their disgrace and shame. God still showed up at the same time as usual for fellowship and communion. But they were nowhere to be found or seen. The enemy had succeeded in causing them to fulfil the lust of the flesh. Notice how when the lust is conceived in our hearts we seek for someone else to corrupt and impart it to or share in our sins. No one wants to have a 'seemingly' good time 'alone' or sin alone.

You gave up, surrendered your self to this, so the blame lies with you and no one else. You entertained, wined and dined it.

Thank God for this wonderful **grace and mercy**, there is a way out of this thing. True repentance must take place in our hearts. God desires you to know him in your heart. We must keep our hearts with all 'diligence'. Guard it against what comes into it and what flows out of it. Don't allow the devil to plant any seeds of evil in your heart, because surely he will watch over it to make sure it grows and matures into what he wants it to become.

Our hearts must be filled in every room with the glory of God. That's why the scripture says, Let this mind be in you which was also in Christ Jesus. We need the mind of Christ; we need to meditate upon the word of God to be pure in our hearts, and to be made whole. As a man thinketh in his heart so is he. Let God's word rule and reign in our hearts so that his word can lead and guide us and so that our 'souls' can prosper.

I'll leave the silver and take the gold. If the silver, the counterfeit appeared to be so good can you just imagine what the Gold will be like. Truly eyes have not seen and ears have not heard. Neither has it entered into the hearts of men, the things that God has prepared for his people, you and I.

What is silver for you, may be gold for someone else! What I saw in my dream was silver. The Gold signifies patience, longsuffering, love, security, understanding, peace. The silver represents the carbon copy, of the real thing. Why take the carbon copy when you can have the original. God does not validate it as the real thing. The 'real thing' or the original document or person has the seal of approval on it, God's seal of approval and his signature and authorisation, on the headed paper. He has the kingdom's authority and God given right to present himself to you. Don't lose out because you couldn't wait.

Love is a driving force and love must be the motive for everything that we do. Love constrains and restrains holds you back and forcibly confines you, restricts severely.

After the Lord delivered me, he gave me a song, My Faith Looks up to thee, thou Lamb of Calvary. But he also put an extra word in at the beginning, which was NOW! Now that all my plans have fallen apart. Now that I realise what I had requested from God was not good enough for me, Now I desire the Bread and what I had asked for was stone. God said to me leave the silver and choose the gold. I have better for you than what you desire. Now that I agreed with God to follow his will and accept what he has for me because, every good gift and perfect gift which is from above cometh down from the Father of Lights with whom there is no variableness nor shadow of turning. Now that I decided that I would no longer deny the power of God moving in my life. Now I agree to surrender and let God have his way. God says Now! After all that's happened my faith is looking up to the Lamb of Calvary. I embrace your will and I trust You, and trust that You know what's best for me, better than I do, and I'll take you at your Word God.

**Prayer of Submission:**

Lord, I repent of my sins, for praying all this time outside of the will of God. I repent for my sins and for denying the truth. I now receive your spirit of acceptance, and receive what your divine will is for my life. Let thy will be done on earth as it is in Heaven in my life. The pattern and design is in Heaven and will be deposited in my heart. Lord from this day forth, I will delight to do your will, in Jesus Name, and no longer linger in yesterday's mistakes, dreams or misfortunes.

Thank you for your choices for my life that I will ACCEPT as my choices, for You choose our inheritance, for us which is the excellency of Jacob. Psalms 47:4.

I love you Lord. I agree with your will and admit that your way is better than mine, and will be very rewarding!

## CHAPTER 7

## SEIZE THE MOMENT!
## TAMAR – 'BREAKING FORTH!'

**Tamar – carrying out a means to justify an end.**

Let us take a walk down to Sister Tamar, Elder Judah's daughter in-law. Our Sister Tamar had just about enough of empty promises. She had taken as much as she could take and it was time for her to take what was due to her.

Sis. Tamar in Genesis 38 is a 'Risk-taker'. First of all, she put her own reputation on the line. Jesus made Himself of no reputation to go to the cross to die for the world.

Tamar was a 'Woman of Valour'. She was strong and courageous, full of faith, operating with speed. She

seized the moment of opportunity. Tamar sensed the
timing, and urgency of the hour and decided not to let
her moment pass by again.

Tamar was a 'Woman of Purpose'. The lineage of Jesus
Christ was to come through Tamar. Judah had given her
two of his sons in marriage, Er and Onan, and both had
died. She had no seed from any of her husbands and
yet the royal seed was supposed to come through her!
Judah had one more son and promised to give him to
Tamar when he was old enough. According to the law
in those days, a man had to do this in order to raise up
seed for his brother. The lineage must be continued for
the purpose of Christ to be born, He was destined to
come through the tribe of Judah, and through Tamar,
God's chosen vessel.

There was a *cause!* This caused her to move quickly
and effectively and out of *desperation* for the promise
of God to be fulfilled in her life. The promise of having
a child. Tamar was barren and in those days it was a
shame for a woman to be married and also barren. It
is my belief that she was moving in obedience to the
Spirit. She discerned her season and time to get what
was rightfully hers. Time was of the essence; the final
hour had come. Tamar had to grasp it, and lay hold on

it firmly with both hands. There was a word that God would bless the fruit of her womb but she did not know how? And since Judah was keeping his only son left from her, it looked impossible. Judah did not keep his word to Tamar. The hearts of her two previous husbands were corrupt and wicked therefore God gave her no seed from them.

The shame that Tamar would have had to bear was unbearable. Imagine everyone talking about her and saying that 'she's had two husbands, she must have done something to them for both of them to be dead. She must be a witch or have a curse on her or something. You know what people are like when they begin to gossip. Tamar carried the shame for so long, and was the talk of the village and everyone's favourite subject in the market place and at breakfast in Harrods.

This could bring about change for Tamar, she had been weeping for a long time but now joy was in sight. She was scarred and wounded, depressed and oppressed by life's cruel gossips and hate mail. Everyone was talking about her. 'There must be something wrong with Tamar's womb. We live in a cruel society and people are unkind. If you become a widow once people can understand, but twice, no something is not right, she must have some sort of curse', and people become suspiscious. The hearts of her late husbands were so wicked that God did not want their evil corrupt ways or hearts to mess up the royal seed, that would come in the generations ahead.

Her second husband was actually spilling his seed on the ground so that his own seed would not bring honour to his dead brother. He was spiteful and broke the law and God killed him for it. He was trying to stop the heavenly order, the plan of God. But did you know that if you try to hinder the move of God, you are just designing your own downfall because God will not let nothing get in the way of His divine plan. Initially the root of the problem was with Judah, as the Israelites had been forbidden to marry outside of their culture. Judah married a Canaanite woman in disobedience to God's word and their laws at that time. (Thank God for liberty now!) Oh you can get away with stuff for a while but woe betide when God decides to execute judgement. Her husband had caused her to be a laughing stock in the streets, the talk of the town, being mocked and jeered and openly embarrassed, and publicly disgraced. She had to watch the other women pushing their push-chairs in the market and shopping center and having their days out at the park and showing off on her. She could not join in the mother and baby talk and shopping trips. She was an outcast from her friends. Friends get married and have children and then they forget they ever knew you! Sound familiar? Boasting in her face! Oh the pain and anguish and longing in her heart to have and hold her very own flesh and blood, her very own baby in her aching, waiting, outstretched arms. Life had been cruel and hard, bitter and painful but now her season to be barren and childless was about to change. Tamar discerned and sensed it.

Tamar's arms longed to hold a baby so badly her heart ached, and her arms ached! Every time she saw someone with a baby her heart skipped a beat. Her heart broke. She longed to rock her own baby in her arms, she had rocked everyone else's. Her nieces and nephews, friends and even strangers, but she always had to give them back at the end of the day, she desired her own baby, and rightfully so. God made husband and wife to reproduce after their own kind, that was the divine heavenly order.

Tamar saw her chance to obtain the promise and her joy back. After-all weeping may endure for a night but joy comes in the morning. Her season was about to change, bless God!

Tamar probably told no one what she was going to do. In order to receive her blessing, she had to obey God's Word that she heard in her heart and spirit. She had to do 'something'. She had to activate her faith, and participate in the performing of God's Word for her life.

Tamar had to do her part. Just like Abraham, God told him that he would have a son, and as old as they were, it was not going to be supernaturally or happen by immaculate conception. No they had to get together and perform their husband and wifely duties, and God gave them the strength to get physical and fleshly in making love, in order for the sperm to meet with the egg and for destiny to meet up head on collision with eternity. It was the only way! So they got sexually active, even in their old age. God opened up Abraham and Sarah's sexual appetite and touched their loins, touched Sarah's reproductive organs, and as they did their part and activated their faith, Jehovah did His. God Kept His Word, and performed the PROMISE to them. A son was born to them, the Son of PROMISE, ISAAC.

## RADICAL OBEDIENCE!

Tamar's faith became a radical act of obedience! She had some *crazy faith*. She took a risk and broke the protocol and the code of the law, in order to be blessed. She broke every rule in the book! God knows that if she had 'laid down' with any other man, she would have been killed, and this is according to the law at that time! Tamar risked her life to obtain the promised seed.

Judah had no intention of giving her his third son as he feared him also dying. So he instructed her to go her father's house to wait for him to grow up, with no intention of keeping his word to her. God had another plan and another way of doing things. God is not mocked. The devil was trying to stop the seed of David, but God intervened, and what the devil meant for evil, God turned it around for good.

Tamar disguised herself, changed her widow garments, and put a veil over her face, dressed like a prostitute and went out into the streets, into the place where she knew he would be. She set out to achieve by other desperate means what belonged to her, and was rightfully hers. It was her inheritance, her future. Tamar carefully planned to obtain something valuable from Judah as proof of his identity, it was a matter of life and death for a single woman. She convinced him to leave his signet ring, bracelet and staff. The three significant things that confirmed his true identity were carelessly given to her as evidence for the future, proving that he was the father of her unborn child. This was her only way to freedom. He made a pledge to return the next day also with a 'kid' for payment, but that would not serve as evidence. Tamar's mission was accomplished.

In doing so, Judah's sin and weakness was discovered, exposed! Tamar had probably heard about Judah's sexual activities and he had probably been doing this for some time. His wife was now dead, so it is possible that he had been seeing other women, prostitutes. May be no one knew anything about it and now he was about to be caught red-handed. Tamar took advantage of his weakness. Through her it was going to be more exposed out into the open. Perhaps this would surely prevent him from continuing in this type of life style. God's strength was made perfect in Judah's weakness. Though Satan tried to stop the heritage, God divinely interrupted through Tamar.

## DOUBLE FOR YOUR TROUBLE!

When the time came for Tamar's pregnancy to be exposed Judah owned up to what he had done and told Tamar that she was more honourable than he, because he did not keep his word to her. Judah could not deny he was the father because she had his signet ring, bracelet and staff as proof, and he had given it to her. He never knew her in that way again. God honoured her because she obeyed Him. God not only honoured her with one son but 'two'. Tamar gave birth to **TWINS!** She received 'double for all her shame, double for her trouble'! Isaiah 61 verse 7, for her years of grief and sorrow and shame. All who saw her would have to call her blessed of the Lord. She had twins – twin boys. The FAVOUR of the Lord was upon her! Grace & Mercy met together and came to her, sought her out and found her. Grace & Mercy endowed her, covered and smothered her and saved her out of all her troubles. Tamar was REDEEMED from her barren state! The weeping was over, and her morning had come.

Tamar received DOUBLE for her TROUBLE! The set time to favour her had come. She received of the Lord's hand, DOUBLE FOR HER TROUBLE! GRACE & MERCY, the undeserved FAVOUR of God! Congratulations you're having *twins!*

We shall receive a Son's Firstborn Inheritance, and when Grace and Mercy comes, we shall receive gifts. Gifts will be released to us! Thank you Jesus!

## QUEEN ESTHER

Esther received double for her trouble, when the king placed the crown upon her head and made her his Queen. She obtained *grace* and *favour* from king Ahaseurus. Esther 2 verse 17-18. Get ready for a **break out** in your life!

### Esther the Orphan

An orphan in today's society, according to the Oxford Dictionary, is a child bereaved of *one* parent or both parents. This means that the child is also bereaved of the protection and the advantages of having both parents.

An orphan is a child who has been abandoned by one of his or her parents or both. If you were brought up by a single parent, you are classified as an orphan! If you were brought up by your grandparents an aunty or an uncle, you are still classed as an orphan. Why? You have been cheated out of being nurtured and loved by loving parents. In the beginning, after God made Adam and Eve, he told them to be fruitful and multiply, to reproduce after their own kind. So the family was designed by God. They increased their family to having two sons, Cain and Abel.

Regardless of how well your grandparents or your aunt and uncle took care of you, or your adopted, foster parents or even the orphanage looked after you, there is always a longing inside of you to seek out and know your birth mother and father. You are always wondering, what they look like, or if your character is anything like theirs.

**Cause & Effect**

Now Esther was an orphan, both her parents were deceased, and her cousin Mordecai took her in and looked after her welfare. Esther 2:7 We don't know at what age she became an orphan, but according to the scripture, it would appear that it happened in her infancy. Whether she lost them at birth or years after being born, it has an emotional effect.

When a child is separated from it's natural mother and from their parents and the family environment, it causes an emotional upset and turmoil, a tearing away of the soul. It's like being ripped apart, from every angle, causing feelings of confusion, distress, depression, insecurity, isolation, low self-esteem. All of their familiar comforts are severed leaving the baby or child empty, lost and surrounded by fear and loneliness. To the child they have been abandoned for no apparent reason. If not well cared for, counselled and given special attention, the child will self-destruct, be disruptive, unsettled and unfriendly.

Imagine how it must have been for Jesus to be separated from his Father, in order to come down to earth, and fulfil his purpose, dying for the sins of the world.

Jesus Christ the Son of God, agreed to be separated from his Father, and go through the things that we have experienced. Many times we think that God doesn't understand but he does, because he went through it himself. He left the splendour, glory and comfort of heaven, stooped low enough, humbled himself to come to us. He knew the pain of being abandoned, as he cried out on the cross, 'Father, why hast thou forsaken me?

We do not know what happened to Joseph, his earthly stepfather, as he is not mentioned after a certain stage in his life. Jesus felt loneliness, he was always going away on his own, in a solitary place to pray to the Father.

Jesus identifies with your pain, he has walked down your street. He is real, he came as a real person in the flesh, and dwelt among flesh. He knew what it was to cry out in anguish and pain for relief from pain. He knew no sin, but became sin. Jesus understands. He was misunderstood just like we were. He was despised and rejected of men, he came unto his own and his own received him not. He understands what it is to be in a single parent home, separation/divorce. Jesus understands.

There may have been times when you tried to contact your family and they didn't want to know you, they couldn't accept you, and they could not forgive themselves for what they had done to you.

It is somewhat inevitable for you not to be bitter and angry when you look back at your past. You feel sorry for yourself and are unable to fit into certain groups because of your past. You may appear to have a bad smell when people of a different type of upbringing are around you.

Like the woman with the 'issue of blood'. Everyone knew her condition. She carried a stench, odour, one of distastefulness. No one would want to identify themselves with her. This woman's sickness kept her in bondage, ostracized, unimportant, out of certain cliques.

People may not want their children to associate with your children because yours are born out of 'wedlock'. Certain couples won't have you around them because you're single or a single parent and you don't come up to their expectations. Friends may leave you when you get divorced, they look on you and who once invited you for dinner, now you can't even hear the telephone ring.

But there is one up in heaven, who sits high and looks low. He looks upon the rejected ones and the despised and forsaken ones. Wrapped up in your shame he's looking at you and loving you all the time. He has a plan and purpose for your life, regardless of how low you've come. You had to come low in order to come up! It's your time!

Esther's time came, when she entered the King's palace, she went straight into her preparation. Her body was being rubbed with different ointments. Six months with one type of ointment six months with different type of ointment.

God had to purge out of her all the bitterness, anger, resentment, ill manners. Healing and deliverance was taking place, she was being 'tamed' from her 'wildness'. Going through a traumatic experience can make one, wild and untamed. The healing process is great and complicated. Your soul has been knocked out of place or alignment and you have to be re-built, re-structured and realigned. This is in itself a task and a half, but not for God. With God all things are possible.

This is done through the many different challenges that we face throughout our lives. We are tested how we handle them, and are put through these tests over and over again until we pass the test. Until you produce the right reaction, behaviour or attitude whilst in a particular situation, God will make you repeat the problem, over and over again.

Now it may be painful, but in the long run, it's for our own good! We are going to the King's Palace, we are quality material and our destiny is one of greatness, therefore it is important that we change our way of thinking, and our reaction to certain things. It's costly, but it will be worth it!

Esther had to learn how to *surrender* to those in authority and leadership positions, as she went through the process of being 'purged'. This was her preparation for the 'blessing' the higher dimension. Esther had no idea that she would soon be the Queen, but God had everything under control, her life mapped out and her destiny tied up in the mess that was going on. She was going through a quick, short, sharp, shock treatment. It was very intense. Esther had to submit under the hand of her supervisors, or she would eventually give up and die spiritually.

It is God's will for you to die to self. Die to your own opinions, and ideas. God expects you to die to your own aspirations, desires, goals. He expects you to rise up to His will and purpose and character. God desires for us to yield our will to His Word and overall rulership over our lives.

When you are in a system that you find difficult to conform to, you will resist the system, and your survival instincts kick in. You feel it necessary to go into self defence. But in order for you to persist and survive in this place, you can make things a lot easier by submitting or surrendering your will, to the will of the system. You won't be able to break the system, the system will break you!

There will be some instances where you react to situations in an abrasive manner. But there are times when you react to a situation and people perceive you to be ill mannered or crazy or something, but it was God putting a spirit of resilience in you, because God is preparing you for where you are going! God wants you to be strong in character as well as submissive.

When we learn to first *submit to God*, the more likely we will be able to submit to authority. Many issues prevent you from submitting at first. But once God shows them to you, make the changes so that you can go forward and jump over every hurdle and become the person that He desires for you to become.

You may have to find some people you have wronged and apologise, or you may have to embrace some people who have rejected you in the past. But whatever it is choose life and live. Go forward, humble yourself and God will exalt you. Humility does not come cheap, it is costly! It will cost you your own self respect and self worth. You may have to lose your identity. It may mean that you have to put your own agenda aside, and put your own way of thinking aside in order to accommodate someone else's. That could be your husband, your employer, your parents or spiritual leaders whatever, but it will always cost you something!

Your ability and agreement to submit to leadership and authority, will determine whether or not you will be able to submit in marriage. If Esther did not learn to submit to those who were in charge of her, then she would never have been able to submit to a King, her husband. God knew exactly what He was doing in her life when he made the way for her to be taken into the Kings Palace and to be chosen at the beauty contest.

Vashti was swiftly removed because of her disobedience to honour her husband's request, even though it was not a sensible one, for he was drunk and his friends, and it was a distasteful and unwise request. But Vashti made her husband look inferior in front of his dignitaries, and this was quite shameful and embarrassing for him.

It may be that Vashti reacted in this way because of the pride that was rooted deep within her heart. It may not have their custom, to have the ladies with the men in this manner. It could be that she had probably been behaving this way in private, but on this occasion it became public knowledge and, it was to cost her, her status, marriage and home! It was a costly mistake, but it was in line with the will of God. A very unwise calculation of behaviour. One that could not under no circumstances be rectified for fear of encouraging this behaviour in other women. Vashti's removal made room for Esther's arrival! Vashti's downfall was Esthers promotion! She was ready and waiting in the wings to take her rightful, *ordained* place. Though Esther did not yet realise it, this was all in the plan and purpose of God. It was the correct timing of God.

Imagine what would have happened to the children of Israel if Joseph had not survived the pit, Potipher's house and the prison. The Israelites would have died in the famine. But he had to learn humility for where he was going, was inside the Kings' Palace. He had to be prepared as he was destined for greatness. He was the 'deliverer' in his time. Moses was the deliverer in his and Esther was the 'deliverer' in this case. Boaz was the 'deliverer' for Naomi and Ruth. Two men were the 'deliverers' for Rahab. Throughout the scriptures, God has always used special ordained men and women to deliver his people out of situations, dilema's or crisis.

It was never about Joseph, it was about the plan and purpose of Almighty God for the nation of Israel. It was never about Rahab, but it was about the 'seed' that was to come through her, after being grafted in from a gentile background. It was never about Esther, it was about God's chosen people, the children of Israel in captivity, who were to be killed at Hamen's signed and sealed legislation, because of one man, Mordecai, not bowing down to him, and he wasn't even the King!

The enemy has always tried to destroy the chosen seed of Israel, could it be that he is trying to destroy you? Don't you dare allow him the opportunity! Stand up and take your rightful place in the Kingdom of God. Discover who you are, and your purpose. Discover the Kingdom of God in you. God's Kingdom needs some more Esthers, more Daniels, more Mordecais. This is the Millenial of the 'Church', God's Kingdom coming on earth, to be ruled and governed by his chosen people!

You could miss your whole purpose for being born, just because you refuse to submit. What a shame! Jesus submitted and went all the way to the Cross. We must be willing to go all the way also, to get to the other side of the Jordan river, where our destiny lies. Go through your Gethesmane experience and allow your flesh to die, so that the will of God comes to the surface and you will surrender to His will. Yield your will and give up totally. Total surrender to the Lord. Just think your whole life depends on your submission. Your children's life depends on your obedience & submission. Could it be that your Church is depending on you to submit to God, before God will release the blessing in your life, and in the lives of His people? Yes it's that awesome! It's all about Him, it's not about you or anyone else and nothing else matters!

Don't miss out on the opportunity to be an awesome woman of God, because of your inability to submit. It is true that we have not been taught how to submit to husbands, or authority, and many of us do not respect authority because of what some authoritarians and leaders or abusive husbands and parents may have done in the past. Abusing their positions for corrupt reasons. But it doesn't change the word of God. It doesn't change God's divine order.

Thank God for His grace and mercy. For His patience and longsuffering with us as women. It just might be that; If Eve had remained submitted to Adam and he had not given up his authority and power, she might not have eaten the forbidden fruit in the 'Garden of Eden'.

Had Ruth not submitted to her mother in-law Naomi, she would not have married Boaz and had the wonderful privilege of being a part of the lineage to Christ.

Had Esther not submitted to the authority of Mordecai, all the children of Israel may have been wiped out.

Rahab and her family would not have been delivered out of Jericho, if she did not humble herself, acknowledge the greatness of the God of the Israelites and plead for her fate. Rahab recognised a *move of God!* She recognized an opportunity for a change to occur in her life. She was fully prepared by God to step out of her past and leave her city and people behind to follow the Israelites. She pleaded for her whole family to be free. Though she was a prostitute by career, there was *virtue* in her.

Will we always be labelled as 'wild' and 'untamed' or will we permit ourselves to go through the process of being humbled, pruned and purged? Will we allow the Lord to make us whole again?

We can agree to submit and receive the gold which is the very best, that God has for us. God has kings for us, if we can just learn humility and divine submission. If we can wait on God and not be anxious, and go through the process, not fix up our own blessing, then surely we shall receive the GOLD, that God has in His *Reserve Bank* for us.

You asked for bread and not stone so take the bread that you can eat, and is tasty, nutritious and gives life! Taste and see that the Lord is good. Leave the silver and choose Gold. Enhance your life! Make God's choice for you, your choice.

# CHAPTER 8

## STAY CLOSE

In Esther chapter 4 we read about Mordecai renting his clothes after hearing what Haman had planned for the Jews. They would all be executed because one man would not bow down to him.

Word was sent to Esther of Mordecai mourning and relenting outside the gates. But because she was distressed about the fact that her husband had not called for her to come to him for thirty days. They had not been close or intimate and because of this she was totally unfocused, and could not initially respond to the situation at hand.

Sometimes you go through trials and in the past I have literally heard the Lord say to me before the trial began 'stay close'. When things begin to happen, it gets harder to pray and read the Bible or worship. You become uncovered and open to spiritual attacks through entertaining a spirit of fear, depression and anxiety. The pain in your heart becomes too difficult to resist or deny and before you know it you are looking for something else to mask that pain.

We begin to nurse our pain and our issues and they come up before God as an idol. Instead of worshiping God we are worshiping our issues. Esther fell into this category when she was neglected by her husband who was being kept busy by the wicked Haman. Haman saw to it that he was drinking every day and spending time with his other concubines.

Esther was a new bride and had been intimate with the King her husband. They had come close enough to each other for the marriage to be consummated and she was now pining for her husband. She was longing for him to hold her in his arms and whisper sweet words in her ear and be close again. She longed for the comfort of his masculine arms and to feel the closeness of his chest. Esther yearned to be intimate with her husband again. She was in pain and had an 'issue'.

Esther sent clothes to cover her cousin Mordecai but he sent a message with a sharp rebuke. His words of sharp rebuke caused her to rise up and focus on the *purpose* of God! Esther needed to get close to God at this time, regardless of her issues. She called for a national prayer and fasting, put on her beautiful robes and went to risk her life to stand before the King without an invitation.

Esther 4:13-14

> *Do not think that because you are in the king's house you alone of all the Jews will escape.*
>
> *For if you remain silent at this time, relief and deliverance for the Jews will arise from another place, but you will perish! And who knows but that you have come to royal position in the palace for such a time as this?*
>
> Esther 4:13-14

Had Mordecai not rebuked Esther strongly, she could have missed the whole purpose for her being in the palace. Thank God that she took heed to the word of God, put her issue aside and arose to the challenge. She shook off every negative thought and words, put her pain aside and took care of God's issue whilst God would eventually take care of hers.

Sisters in Christ I encourage you to rise up to the purpose of God. You can become intimate again with God. It's not over yet, you may be cast down but you are certainly not defeated. You may feel like you have been pressed beyond measure and stretched to the end of your tether, but God is waiting on you to deliver the precious people of God out of their captivity and into their God given liberty. People are waiting on you to get it together and do all that God has purposed in His heart for you to do. Stay close to God through prayer, intercession, praise and thanksgiving.

Lay aside every weight, be strong and of good courage, put on the shield of faith, shake the dust off your shoes and start running. It's your time to be used mightily of God in his kingdom, in this last move of God.

## CHAPTER 9

# WHEN JESUS SITS DOWN!

I am sure that we all know the story of the woman of Samaria in St. John 4. That woman is you today!

Imagine, Jesus sent his disciples away from the scene of his confrontation with the Woman of Samaria, because they would have been a hinderance to the move of God at this point.

This is a woman who was living in shame and with rejection from the other ladies in the community, because of her 'worthless' reputation. This disheartened woman, was ostracised, alone, and had lived with different men and some could have even been married men. This woman was the ladies gossip column at afternoon tea and on the way to the well!

I wonder how many times, and for how long she must have dragged herself to the well to get her supply of water, knowing that she was not accepted by the other women, and that she could not go at the same time as the other women, as they would have probably cursed her and called her names, and ostracised her. Rejected by the other reputable married women and single women of Samaria, she was a 'loner'. Friendless, helpless, and despised. Her reputation was in shreds, may be through her own fault and her wreckless way of living. Or may be through 'unforeseen' circumstances, that she had no control over. How many women in times past and today give up their bodies for the sake of a loaf of bread and a pint of milk, a few pounds in the gas metre and a few pounds on the electricity key.

Surely the day would come when the need deep down on the inside of her would be filled. How much longer could she go on doing the things that she no longer found pleasure in, but did not know how to put an end to her misery. All she really wanted was the peace and joy of the Lord. Her life was filled with the guilt and 'shame', of her past and present situation. She walked with her head down on the ground and her feet shuffling along the street in total confusion. Pain surrounded her life, her heart was broken and devastated and hope had gone healing was nowehere in sight for her. Her life's dreams had been broken, and her will to continue living was running thin..

Jesus set himself up to meet with this same woman. It was a 'divine appointment'. One that could not be interrupted, her whole life was about to change. She was about to receive, healing, deliverance, purpose, destiny. The change of season had come for her and Jesus was not about to pass her by because of the body-guards around him, no. He must divert their attention elsewhere. A quick work was to be done. He knew her schedule and decided to come and *sit down and wait for her to come*. The way had been cleared. All the resistance, and hinderances had been removed.

A new move of God was about to happen! Salvation was coming to the Samaritans through a woman of God. A woman who was broken and was about to be healed, blessed and used of God in a mighty way. The army of the Lord was about to arise to a new dimension! Jesus was in the area for a change to occur!

Jesus sat down by the well watching the direction from which she would come, **waiting** for this 'divine appointment'. It reminds me of the times when my father would sit down and wait for us to come home from School, by the front door looking at his 'watch'.

Sometimes we go astray, or we get distracted from what God has told us to do. It may be that God was just putting you through some sort of test, to see how far you would go with Him. May be you have had to give up something or someone that you really loved, in order to prove your love for someone else, God. God wants first place in your life, He will not be second best. He must be first in your heart.

But I bless God, to know that He sits down at 'the place' and **waits** patiently for us to come back to the place where we left off. Thank God for mercy and grace and divine favour. He could have fired us and used someone else but He gives a second and third and fourth chance to get it right. Thank you Jesus. Sometimes we are looking for God to move one way and He comes in another way. It may not be pleasing to us but God loves us and said I chasten every child, and that we should not feint when He does.

Perhaps you used to serve the Lord, or you have been previously used of God and you were cast down, discouraged or even intimidated and left your place of serving. God wants to put you back together again and use you for His glory, if you will obey, humble yourself and yield to the leadership and authority of the Holy Spirit. We must not fight to control our lives, and to be God over our lives. Our lives are hid in Christ Jesus, it is not our life. He is our God and King. Resentment and anger will build up in your heart if you can not forgive those who have hurt you! Allow God to pour in the oil and wine and heal you.

When Jesus said to the woman, 'Give me to drink!' He was not asking her a favour, or a question! Jesus was demanding from her what belongs to him. That is her praise, her glory, her worship. Give unto the Lord, the glory due unto his name, Psalms 29:1. He was saying give Me your worship, not these men who don't love you enough to marry you, and make an honest woman of you. Give me your attention. I can give you what you need, what it is your soul longs for. Life and peace and rest and healing, I can give you that abundant life that your soul so desires.

God created us to praise him. He said *this people have I formed for myself, they shall show forth my praise.* If we don't praise God, we will praise something else. God is a jealous God, and he is jealous over his people. Praise belongs to God.

Worship is the adoration of who He is, and once you have learnt to praise then it is only natural that you would feel the need to go further into His presence and WORSHIP Him, at His footstool. Worship demands your full attention and focus to be upon God.

Jesus said to her, now is the time for the true worshipers to come and *worship the Father in spirit and in truth.* He had come to realign her thoughts and to readjust her. To line her up correctly with the word of God. Line upon line, precept upon precept. In order to go to the next level, Jesus had to spend time with this woman in order to change her focus, the way in which she saw things and her beliefs. Her eye sight was from the wrong angle. 'Our fathers worshiped in the mountains'. Jesus needed to change her thought pattern and perception. She was going to another level, a new dimension, a shifting was about to take place in her life and He must prepare her for the new 'assignment'. Thank God that He takes time out for us when others won't, for He alone is our Saviour and focal point. In order for her to go to a new dimension, her vision must 'change'. Jesus came to her that day to launch her into her purpose, into her destiny. She was destined for greatness and she did not realise it. This was her day! She was to become one of the greatest Evangelist that ever lived. 'Come **see** a man. Is not this the Christ?'

The message that this woman brought to the Samaritans was believed because of the Word that she spoke. Out of her belly was flowing rivers of living waters, now that she had received salvation, spiritual drink from the Lord. Isn't that powerful! Some believed because of the signs and wonders, and some because they heard him for themselves. Nevertheless, Jesus broke the rules again, by speaking to a woman who was not fully Jewish, and by giving the gospel to a **woman** to preach across the nation!

As Jesus sits and waits for us to come into our rightful places, I pray that everyone who reads this book will begin to ask the Lord am I in my rightful place? Or am I just biding my time? Please listen, you cannot give birth to your miracle, if you are not where you are supposed to be.

## Hard Labour

Micah 4:10-13 (Amplified version)

> *Writhe in pain and labour to bring forth, O Daughter of Zion, like a woman in childbirth (travail) for now you shall go forth out of the city and you shall live in the open country. You shall go to Babylon; there you shall be rescued. There the Lord shall redeem you from the hand of your enemies'.*

One Sunday morning the Holy Spirit led me to stay home and pray. As I began to pray an anointing was released to pray and I heard the Lord say well done when I was through. But then I suddenly went into travail, and I felt terrible pain in my lower abdomen and the lower part of my back. As I lay on the floor travailing, I saw myself lying on a hospital bed (trolley more like) and my stomac was open with the head of a baby literally sticking out. A nurse was standing a short distance away from the bed, but no one was actually attending to me. I started to cry saying 'don't leave me here like this'. I heard the voice of the Lord say to me, 'I AM coming!

The 'position' that I was in left me helpless an unable to do anything at all. There is no way that I could get up or do anything for myself.

The position that you may find yourself in right now may be uncomfortable and painful, and you may not know how to get to the place where you know God has ordained for you to be. But be in pain and labour to bring forth! Holler if you have to, scream if you have to, shout if you have to, but don't keep quiet. Women in labour don't keep silent, make some sort of *noise*.

Praise, pray, cry, sing and intercede. Sometimes you just have to sit still and let the Holy Spirit minister to you.

God is coming, he is on his way to bring you out of that situation, He will not leave you in that state. He has invested too much in you to leave you. His purpose must be fulfilled in your life. Do not abort the baby. Do not abort your miracle. Do not abort your PURPOSE. No way! No-how! Don't give up and die, regardless of how desperate your situation may be, God says I am coming to deliver and redeem you out of your situation. Just like he came for Rahab, and Ruth, Hannah, the woman of Samaria, and Rebecca the wife of Isaac.

Rahab a prostitute, saw a way out of her situation and the instructions that were given to her by the spies, was tie the red piece of thread to the window, and we will get you out. Rahab had to obey the instructions given to her by the spies, Joshua 2:18. Our **obedience** to the voice of the Lord will be the way out of the situation that seems to be holding us down right now! The simple instructions that God has given you, if you obey, it will lead to the light, entrance of our blessing! It will lead to the opening of the great door that has been opened for us in heaven and on earth. We must go through the 'door'. Fight with all your might to obey the WILL of the Lord. Surrender to his WORD, yield yourself over to Him. We must walk by faith and not by sight. The things that we see are only 'temporal', they will fade away with the wind.

Babylon is a place where there is strife, confusion, disorder, disillusionment and it is a place where you have had disappointment perhaps in times past. Babylon is where you've had a failed marriage, unequally yoked relationships, lived in sin and experienced emotional pain and damage. You may have experienced rape, molestation, drug abuse, abandoned, and left for dead but it is the place and point where you must go back to, in order to pick up the shattered pieces of your life, gather them together and bring them before the Lord and press on upward.

Babylon is that place where friends walked out on you, families turned their backs on you and you suffered much loss, much pain. In the spirit realm, you are placed in Babylon and it's surroundings are like being in the bottomless pit of hell. There is much travail, much perseverance in the spirit needed in order to get through and out of Babylon.

In the spiritual place of Babylon, there is resentment, hatred, jealousy, envy, rejection, covetousness, betrayal, offenses and unforgiveness, bitterness and depression. These control the city gates and in order for you to go through and come out victorious, you will have to face all of these doorways.

A 'great door' has been opened unto me but there are many adversaries. (Acts 16:9)

Pray and ask God to shed his love abroad in your heart when the offenses come. It is essential that you don't become stuck at this point. This was the hardest hurdle for me. This obstacle caused me to stumble, big time!

Here everything I knew about the love of God was put on trial. When the offense strikes it is very sharp and has a chilling effect! It is like being cut open on an operating table, without being given an anaesthetic. Every attitude in you comes gushing out, your speech and behaviour just becomes ugly and bitter. You upset people around you and don't know why. You scream and holler, sing and pray and it does not appear to get any better.

Thank God He won't leave us there in that wretched state. At this point and time of our lives it is important to understand that God still loves you, no matter how you feel, or how ugly your behaviour gets. It seems like you will never get past the offense but hold on to God, He will deliver you out from this uncomfortable state.

Jesus Christ surrendered his flesh as a 'perfect sacrifice'. He yielded up the ghost, went down into the ground, burst through the gates of hell, ie. resentment, murder, bitterness, anger, unforgiveness, fear, strife and jealousy, hate, pride and took the keys to the Kingdom and the power of the Love of the Father, resurrected him from the grave, and pit of hell. No power of hell could hold his body down because he conquered hell with the Love of God. Love covers a 'multitude of sins'.

When Rachel, the mother of Joseph was in labour with her second son Benjamen, the Bible says that she had **hard labour.** But the midwives told her (Genesis 35:18),

*'Fear not you will have this baby!'*

I received this very same scripture one morning, but did not know what it meant. However, I rejoiced over the part that said, 'fear not you will have this baby!' I rejoiced over it because I thought however long it takes and whatever happens I am going to have my miracle, my vision will come to pass. But I was in for a great shock to my system, as I had no idea what I would have to go through.

Imagine you could get to a place where you actually love the woman who took your husband and split up your marriage, separated your children from their father. Imagine loving the thieves that stole your credit cards and emptied your bank account. Imagine showing love to the bank manager who repossessed your house! Imagine loving the people who intimidated you and forced you to leave your ministry or the company where you worked so hard for your promotion. Imagine showing love to your enemies and feeding them and sincerely praying for them.

'Remember that we are instructed in the Word of God to 'Bless them that hate you and do good to those who despitefully use you', Matt 5:44. These are not only words written in the Bible but they must be written upon the table of our hearts and put in to action. It must be expressed in our every day lives. The Kingdom of Heaven suffereth violence and the violent take it by force, Matt 11:12. Force your way through every pain and suffering, push through resentment and anger, push past malice and pride and grab a hold of CHRIST and let the power of HIS love bring you through in VICTORY over these setbacks.

You of your self could not love them, but the love of Jesus Christ shed abroad in your heart can. It's not your love it's Christ's love. Owe no man anything but LOVE, Romans 13:8. Sounds hard doesn't it? But it is possible and needful in order for us to truly gain Christ. To suffer with Christ is to identify with Him, so that His glory is revealed. It will be worth it all in the end, for the latter shall be greater than the former. You will receive a great harvest, an abundance of love, joy, peace, righteousness. You will receive the Spirit without measure!

# CHAPTER 10

## SECOND CHANCE

In the book of Jonah we are told about a Prophet of God who was most disobedient to the 'specific instructions' that the Lord had given to him concerning his *purpose* in the great City of Ninevah. He spent time in the presence of the Lord where the Will of God for his life was revealed to him by the Spirit.

Jonah rose up to flee from the presence of God and his *purpose* unto another location, totally against the Will of God. The Ninevites were not Jews, and perhaps Jonah wanted to go to his own people. May be Jonah wanted to stand in the pulpit and preach the word where everyone he knew could see him being used by God. Or preach in the streets of his home town where he was better known. He certainly did not want to go to a place where no one knew who he was.

We can not tell God how and when or where He must use us. Our lives are in God's hands and His will for our lives comes before our will. Jonah presumptuously took off, hoping to abort the purpose of God for his life, only to end up in the bottom of the sea, in the belly of a 'great fish'.

Did you know that you can be the main cause for the *storm* that is in your life right now! Your disobedience to God can cause you to be in a trap that there seems to be no way out of. Jonah went to sleep in the ship not knowing that a storm had even come. Strong gusty winds were blowing and he was not at all disturbed.

The other men on the ship threw overboard very precious cargo in order to lighten the ship, and whilst they panicked Jonah slept. He was the reason for the problem yet he was *asleep*. When you step out of the Will of God you go to sleep spiritually, and lose your sense of direction. It is as though you are hanging by a thread even though you don't know it. It's just the mercies of God that's keeping you right now. Thank God that He is patient with us and longsuffering, otherwise God would have cut us off a long time ago.

## Pride

Jonah represents many people in the Church today. *Pride* is the underlying root of all sin whether we want to agree or not. How can we stand up to God and say I'm not doing what you said? I refuse to obey you! I have other things I want to do. This is the flesh kicking in, to hinder us from doing what God said. We put our own human intellect before the Word of God and we make a decision to follow our human intellect and not the Spirit. of God. Then we end up in confusion and rebellion against the Word of God.

We need to cast down every 'imagination' and every 'high thing' that exalts itself against the *knowledge of God* and bring every **thought** into captivity, unto the obedience of Christ.

The higher the calling on your life, is the more the devil will fight you, causing you to resist God sometimes without fully realising it. You can think that you are so right when you are so wrong. Humble yourself under the mighty hand of God. Submit yourself to the WORD of God and to those that have the rule over you. Pride comes before destruction a haughty spirit before a fall. Jonah was striving against God and God said 'My Spirit will not always strive with man!'

'Except a corn of wheat fall into the ground and die, it abideth alone'.

The **corn of wheat** represents our human 'flesh'. The greatest challenge we have in life is against our flesh that fights for control of our lives. This is why it is important for us to line up our thoughts on a daily basis with the Word of God. It is essential for us to seek the mind of Christ. Let this mind be in you, which was also in Christ Jesus. The Word of God must dwell in us 'richly', so that we can discern between right and wrong, truth and untruth, good and evil.

We are so 'sensitive' today because we are too fleshly. Everything upsets us and we are so very easily offended. This is hindering us in our daily walk with God. The first thing we do when we are offended is say; 'I'm not coming back to Church'. Why? God did not offend you. Then we decide to keep 'malice' against our brethren. God is not pleased with our attitude and we must change, not God. Forgive quickly and agree with your brother quickly. Don't let the sun go down on your anger. Free yourself and do not allow yourself to be entangled again in the **yoke of bondage.** It hinders your praises, your prayers and the move of God in your life. Live and let live and agree to disagree. Love even when it hurts. That's the time to show love, when it hurts you.

Christ was wounded for our transgressions, He was bruised for our iniquities, the chastisement of our peace was upon him and by his stripes we are healed, Isaiah 53:5.

You don't have time to walk around in bitterness, anger and offense it will consume you!

So when offenses come we disobey God, we blame God and take it out on God and we harm ourselves. This is not the way God desires for you to live.

Be strong in the Lord and the power of His might. Put on the whole armour of God and stand against the wiles of the devil. For we wrestle not against flesh and blood but against principalities, Ephesians 6:10.

We are in a war, a spiritual battle. But we are fighting the wrong person when we fight our brethren. We are to fight against the devil and his agents. Again I say BE STRONG you mighty warrior of God!

It is amazing to me that Jonah would ask the shipmaster to throw him overboard into the sea, without first desiring to call upon God. He wished to die rather than do the will of God. But God was not through with Jonah. God strategically prepared a great fish to swallow him up so that He could really deal with the main problem, his **'flesh'**.

The only way out of the belly of the fish was Jonah's repentance which first took place in his heart. Jonah remembered his vow that he had made to the Lord before he got into that situation. As the Holy Spirit convicted him in his heart, he came to himself and prayed to the Lord promising to pay his vow unto the Lord. At this point, after 3 days in the belly of the fish, he was ready to go and do the will of God. He surrendered to God, humbled himself, cried out to God and God forgave him for his disobedience but allowed him to now follow the previous instructions of the Lord.

When we get tired of running away from the will of God and following our own desires, God will be able to use us. You can only run for a time. You are fighting a losing battle if you are fighting against the will of God. He will allow affliction to come upon you, he will cause you to fall into situations that only He can deliver you out from, until you say YES to the Lord, and agree to be obedient to God's perfect will.

Let your flesh die. Die to your own desires, ambitions and leave the silver. Leave your ambitions, ideology, plans that you have for your life and accept the plan of God. Chooose GOLD, it's God's way. Choose LIFE and LIVE. Choose the WILL OF GOD!

# CHAPTER 11

## 'FLESH' – 2 RAVENS AND A BROOK.

I Kings 17

Elijah the Tishbite and great prophet of God was a radical man of God. He can be viewed as an extremists! He commanded that there be no rain on the earth. Water is essential not only for people, but for nature. To feed the animals, trees and forests, land, agriculture etc.

Notice Elijah's words: 'As the Lord liveth, there will be no rain until I say so'. Elijah used his influencial position to manipulate God to move on his say so. God honours the word in the prophets mouth. God did not send Elijah to Ahab. Elijah had a passionate heart for God and he allowed his anger to get the better of him. His strong passion, the fire in him was not tamed. It was wild and untamed. His zeal was his downfall and caused him to fall into error. This is why God told Elijah to hide himself. Elijah's flesh was not yet under subjection.

God used ravens, crows, birds that eat dead animals. Rotting meat, repulsive. They are scavengers and God used them to feed Elijah 'rations'. This was God's provision for Elijah in the wilderness, a lonely place. A brook was there for water and 'roar flesh' for food. Eagles eat fresh meat, live prey but ravens eat dead things.

The 'flesh' that Elijah was being fed with represents some of us today having to buy food in shops like Netto's or Kwik-Save instead of Sainsbury's, Marks & Spencers, or Tesco's.

The 'flesh' represents us having to buy our clothes in the market instead of Harrods or Selfridges.

The 'flesh' represents us having to scrounge through the sales to get the best possible bargain, not because you want to save money, but because you just couldn't afford it otherwise.

The 'flesh' represents going to Butlins for holidays instead of DisneyWorld or somewhere exotic like Barbados, Jamaica, places of paradise.

The 'flesh' represents having to use meal tickets, food vouchers in order to get rations instead of being able to buy plenty and being spoilt for choice. Eating left-overs, wearing hand-me-downs instead of being able to have the free will / choice of what to buy or where to shop.

The 'flesh' represents driving a banger for a car instead of the top range, living less than the life of children of the King.

The 'flesh' represents having the world system dictate to you how the Schools should be run, what your chilldren should be taught.

The 'flesh' represents the junk that comes on television being fed by the world media, newspapers, filth, pornography. 'FLESH'.

The 'flesh' represents not having any money to pay your bills barely surviving struggling to make ends meet. Scavengers – when you finish eating, the crows come back for the leftovers from your plate! So they came twice a day. This state is that of some people in the church today. We are living below our means.

The Church is in transit right now. It's moving from a place of disobedience to a place of obedience. A time of disobedience to a time of 'total obedience'. A quiet place of rest. It's a wealthy moist place. In a healthy environment the church is going to be placed in it's rightful place beside the bridegroom. The Church, the bride of Christ is about to be engaged by the King, her husband. We engage you Lord Jesus Christ our Saviour and the bride will move alongside the bridegroom, at the same time as her Lord and master. We the Church will move in the spirit of agreement with oneness of mind and spirit, in total cooperation and submission to the husband, Christ the Lord. Side by side, one step at a time.

# CHAPTER 12

## AGREEMENT

In Ezekiel 1, the angels wings were linked, engaged to one another. They were in position. The angels wings, wheels, faces on all four sides (4 = establishment in the four corners of the earth). They all move at the same time in sychronisation to the Spirit of God. The Spirit was in the wheels and they were being led by the Spirit of God. The fire, the cloud was the result of the movement of the presence of God. It was a 'higher dimension'. A spirit of *agreement* and harmony will be in God's people. You see God's glory and the affect after He has moved. This is the time for the body of Christ to begin to move in *agreement* to God's word. The GLORY of GOD IS COMING. The bride will go wherever the bridegroom leads it to go. They will move in harmony, unity, peace, strength and perfection.

The Church will have 'straight feet' and will move 'straight forward' in accordance to the will of God. The soles of the feet of the Church will have sweet flavourings in it and will leave a devastation as it moves in the earth. It will cause a disruption and destruction to the kingdom of darkness, wherever it moves or goes. Signs and wonders, healing, deliverance and restoration it will most certainly bring.

We will fold our human intelligence, human reasoning of the mind and spirit and follow after the Spirit of God. **Devastation, destruction and demolition** of the devil's kingdom will be on the streets and we will run to catch up with God.

There'll be no distraction as the Church will be realigned in order to be able to move in total agreement and in **synchronisation** with the Spirit of God. As it is in Heaven, so will be done on earth. When the Spirit of God is moving the Church will move at precisely the same time in agreement of His Spirit. The Church must change it's own perceptions to a spirit of complete *acceptance* to what God says. Just accept what God is dong and move with it. The true bride of Christ won't turn back again and go back into rebellious state. Ultimately, the Church will move obedient and triumphantly and she shall be 'caught up' to be with the Lord. The 'catching away' of the bride of Christ is soon to come. The watchmen of the body of Christ will *look out* and see the move of the Spirit they shall see with *sharp eyes* and *total vision*. She shall have sharp vision with the correct tools, deeper insight and be well equipped with the pure, undiluted, unadulterated, uncompromising word of TRUTH.

Elijah was instructed by God to go back and show himself to King Ahab. A man who was under the power of the spirit of influence operating through his wife, Jezebel. The rebellious Church that has been living in fear, under the oppression of the spirit of control and power of influence.

When God gets through with his people, the atmosphere and temperature will be set to His desired control. It will be God's Spirit and power that comes into manifestation as he returns to dwell among his people. God will take control of the thermostat. We keep on turning God on and off but He will come and take his rightful place in our hearts, and in his Church and He will dwell among us and walk up and down among us, and He will be *our God, who will rule and reign supreme!*

Elijah was sent to release the rain which he had caused to stop at his word. God humbled him and it was a humbling experience to be fed by the black scavenger ravens. His spirit was tamed. NOW he was ready for a 'higher dimension'. He was GOLD tried in the fire, prepared and ready for the next level.

**The Next Level**

The next level is wrapped up in one word, OBEDIENCE. A 'step by step' instruction given by the Lord asking Him, can I go here or can I go there! Seeking God in everything we do, every move we make, every decision we make. It's God's WAY or no 'way'. We are not our own, just simply called to move in accordance with the Spirit of the living God.

Elijah had been in a place where he had to learn to become totally dependent upon God. There he would have experienced loneliness, as he was cut off from society. There was no television, no-one to converse with. Just himself and God. There were no telephones, no letter writing he was just alone.

During this time Elijah would have sought the Lord, repented, amended his ways and died to his flesh. God was teaching him also patience, endurance, longsuffering, obedience, trust. To listen to God and to *know* His voice. He was being prepared for the next level, full time ministry. Some time after this Elijah was teaching and managing a school of prophets.

Elijah received a *greater anointing* in order for the task that lay ahead. All the time that he was by the Brook Cherith, people were waiting on him. His time and season had now come to move up higher in God and to move out into destiny. Elijah moved out from insignificance to significance. Elijah was destined to affect the world.

## PAY YOUR VOWS

If you made the Lord a promise like we do when we are in trouble. We say 'Lord if you get me out of this one, I'll serve you for the rest of my life. But after God does it we quickly forget what we promised God.

Jephthah vowed to give God the first thing that came out of his house to meet him, if God would allow him to win the fight against the Ammonites, Judges 11:30-40. He did not know that the most precious and closest thing to his heart, his daughter, would be the one to come running through the doors to welcome him home and rejoice in his God given victory over the enemy. May be he had not thought about it properly, before making the vow, but he had to honour his word / vow to God.

## The Power of Agreement

The amazing and wonderful beauty about the daughter of Jephthah, is that she did not argue with her father or resist him. She did not go rebel or against the will of her father whom she loved and respected fully. She would honour his headship and authority.

Jephthah's daughter demonstrated her love for her father by **agreeing** to fulfil the promise or the vow that he had made to God. What love, what loyalty and honour this shows on her part. What a sacrifice this would be for her! She was never to be married, but she would give herself and lay down her life for full time ministry, because of the words uttered out of her father's mouth to God.

This is the type of agreement that God is looking for from us. If we look at Jephthah as our Father God, and see his daughter as representing the bride of Christ, who is the Church, then we can see that God desires for the Church to be in agreement with the head of the Church, which is Christ. When He speaks he expects us to move in obedience to his word and in full agreement and submission. This is the internal beauty of the bride, that she is totally committed to the bridegroom and has total respect, love, honour and loyalty for Him.

This was a costly sacrifice! Jephthah wished that he could turn the clock back, and that he had not opened his mouth unto God, but it was too late. The painful thing about this vow is that his daughter was his only child. This means that he would have no grandchildren, and no other children to carry on his name. Indeed a *costly sacrifice!*

There is a call in the Spirit for you to fulfil your promise to God. What was it you promised the LORD. Have you stayed true to your word?

## CHAPTER 14

# THE PERFECT SACRIFICE

Wise men brought gifts unto Jesus. What was the cost of the gift. What price did they pay in order to obtain or purchase those gifts and look how freely they gave their best gift to the child, King Jesus! They offered GOLD, frankincense and myrrh. These are all costly gifts. I wonder what they had to suffer in order to gain these gifts?

David said, 'I will not offer that which costs me nothing', and paid 50 pieces of silver for his sacrifice to offer up to the Lord. God wants something from you that cost you something. It is something that's meaningful to you. It may hurt to give it up but it's what God desires. It may be something that you hold most precious to your heart. It's the 'perfect sacrifice'. A sacrifice that says

'Lord I am grateful for what you've done for me, so I bring you my very best gift.

What do you have to bring to the Lord?

What do you have to offer God.

He wants your **best gift.** Nothing else and nothing less will do!

The woman with the Alabaster Box of sweet, precious ointment. What did she give up in order to afford her precious gift, the oil in her Alabaster box? We will never know, but it was costly! She paid a price for it, it did not come easily. It was her blood, sweat and tears that got her that oil, yet she parted with it in order to carry out the purpose of God. She sensed a move of God, she was in tune to the timing of the Spirit, for Christ's head and feet to be anointed with her precious oil before his crucifixion.

This woman was truly grateful to God in her heart, for what he had done in her life and in the life of her brother, Lazarus. This was the 'perfect sacrifice' that God desired and she was willing to give it up! It was costly, valuable, and meaningful.

What are you prepared to give? Has God asked you to give something or someone up for his Son Jesus Christ? It could be your dreams, ideas, your vision, your ambitions or aspirations, your achievements, your career, your family ties. It's costly. Bring your best gift to the Lord. The one that He desires, the one He asked you for. No other gift will do for this specific purpose.

Whatever you refuse to give up for God, eventually you will lose it anyway. Obedience is better than sacrifice.

# CHAPTER 15

## THE PRODIGAL SON'S INHERITANCE!

The Prodigal Son is a perfect example of some us today. He ended up in a place prepared for him by God because he had entered into God's **permissive will,** and not God's **perfect will'**.

He asked his father for just a **portion** of his inheritance and his father granted him his request. Thank God that the father wisely gave him only a portion of his inheritance otherwise he would have blown the whole lot. But his father decided to test him and see if he would apply what he should have learnt from his father, and from being in a stable and respectable home, having a healthy and wealthy background.

It became obvious that the son had not applied what he had learnt or heard in service, or from his father, to his life. His relationship with his father was not quite right. It needed some adjustments. He was so full of pride that he asked his father for his inheritance, he had no patience to wait for the right time when he would have come to maturity in order to handle his inheritance, at which point his inheritance would have been given to him. He clearly did not know what his inheritance was for. He spent his finances within no time at all. He did not invest his finances; he did not give to charity or help someone in need! He did not pay tithes and offering but he decided to squander the lot. He had no knowledge or wisdom of handling his finances nor did he *seek to know*. He asked, and it was given, but he did not seek in order to find or consider knocking. There is a process to receiving, but the prodigal son wanted to go through the short cut. A short cut to prosperity and success. All play and no work!

In the 'prepared place', the pig's pen, specially prepared for him by God, after a period of time came to his physical human senses & human spirit. His human senses had to come to the **realisation** and **actualisation** of the fact that he was not in his rightful place. This was not God's perfect divine will for his life. He realized that his father had a better place *at home* for him.

He was agreed in his spirit and mind with the Spirit of God that it was time to repent, turn around from his own way, and go God's way, which is the way that his father wished for him to go.

There is **Power in Agreement.** Your spirit, in agreement with God's Spirit, moving in the things of God and in the realms of the Spirit.

The prodigal son at this point allowed himself to go through a humbling experience in his spirit and mind. Psalms 51 clearly states that 'a broken spirit and a contrite heart, God will not despise'. He was already broken, and at his lowest level, he couldn't get any lower. He was under his situation.

# CHAPTER 16

## THE ANOINTING DESTROYS THE YOKE

Isaiah 10:27 –

*'Because of the anointing the yoke shall be destroyed'!*

The anointing is the divine presence and overflow of the Power of God that gives authority and unction to destroy yokes, removes burdens and releases a stream of joy.

This anointing empowers us to do what God has called us to do. No matter how big or how small a task. From cleaning the Church to living for Christ, the Christ way.

The situation that the *prodigal* found himself in was evidently a yoke is his life that needed to be destroyed. No one was going to come and deliver him, but God would empower him alone in order that he could receive the power of God to destroy the yoke, through the anointing of God.

The *prodigal son*, through the anointing of God came to his senses; to realize that this is not God's will for his life. He *accessed the power of God* that had been released upon him, repented in his heart; light flooded his heart and enlightened his mind, which caused him to arise from his disposition, and position himself correctly in the direction of home.

As he moved in obedience to the Spirit of God, he sensed that his deliverance had come, and moved in accordance with the timing of the Spirit and set himself to return to his father's home. He was returning home a broken man, filled with **humility**. The Word of God had come to him and he knew in advance what he had to say to his father and how to approach him and it would be completely differently to the attitude he had before he left.

The father's love was drawing him, pulling him, wooing him back to his rightful place. The love of the father was waiting for him. All things would be made bright and beautiful. He thought that on his return the most he would receive was a house servants 'rations' or provision, not knowing that God had a much greater plan and reward for him, for his obedience.

The loving open arms of the father awaited him. There was a greater inheritance waiting for him on his return, but he did not know of this. He did not know that humility is the key to the favour of God!

As he moved in obedience, every step he took to get home got brighter, the burden became easier, because he had now taken an easy yoke and a lighter burden, and was now willing to learn from his father the right way.

His father gave him new shoes, representing a new destiny and purpose for his life. He gave him a ring which signifies the authority and power given to him by his loving father and a new coat. This coat signifies the spirit of humility. He had been **processed** for the greater blessing.

This time he would seek his father's advice and counsel on what to do with his finance. He would not make decisions without consulting him. He would be led every step of the way by his father. He would ask what to do with the finances this time. He would have a heart of compassion by now and would agree to building a home of shelter for the homeless, and providing food for the hungry. He would have a heart for souls for the kingdom of God because he had learned by experience what it was like to suffer loss, pain and heartache.

He was a vessel fit for the master's use. A vessel of mercy! Prepared in the furnace of the fire, purified seven times.

We must obey the instructions of the Lord in order to get back into the perfect will of God. All that glitters is not gold. We need to be in our rightful places in order to receive what God has for us. We need to have the right frame of mind and be humble in order for us to be able to serve God in the way that He desires and for God to be able to serve us in this final hour of restoration for the Church.

Everything God promised for us is waiting for us. It's waiting for us to develop to the level of maturity in order for us to receive the blessing from God. It does not just depend on our paying of tithes and offerings, but it lies heavily dependent upon our obedience to the personal instructions that God gives us for our lives. We try so hard to avoid doing this because our spirit, heart and mind is not in agreement with God's will for us.

God's plan and desire for us is so much better than ours! I choose to surrender now, I am well and truly tired of my own way and I trust that you also will realise that God's way is the only way! He is not only the way, but he is the truth and the life!

Proverbs 23 verse 23 instructs us to;

> 'Buy the truth and sell it not, also wisdom, knowledge and understanding'.

We must part with something in order to gain the wisdom of Christ, his knowledge and understanding. We must walk in the light of his WORD. We are the children of light and therefore we must demonstrate that light and make a conscious decision not to walk in ignorance or darkness.

Christ came that we might have life and that we might have it more abundantly, and He is able to do exceeding abundantly, above all that we can ever ask or think.

Truly eyes have not seen and ears have not heard, neither has it entered into the hearts of men, the things that God has in store for them that love Him.

Go on, take a leap of faith and CHOOSE GOLD.

Please pray with me!

Dear Father, in the name of Jesus, I humble myself under the mighty hand of God and I agree with your Word for me. I comply with the will of God for my life and I repent for going my own way and doing things on my own, my way. I turn my heart towards you God. I turn my heart back to the heart of God, my father, in Jesus name.

I leave the silver and choose Gold in the name of Jesus Christ. I choose your will and desire for me and I choose to trust you and take you at your WORD, in Jesus Name. Amen!

## CHAPTER 17

## SUBMISSION

The next level is 'submission'. It's all about submission, because it speaks of 'marriage'. The marriage must now take place to the King, *Christ and his bride.*

Esther was chosen because of her inner beauty, which was absolutely glowing on the outside. It was a 'glorious beauty'. God has prepared a glorious church without spot or wrinkle.

The 'marriage' of the bridegroom, Jesus and the *bride* of Christ, the church, (wise virgins) must come to reality. The bride of Christ must now come to the forefront and take her place at the table, in the very presence of the 'King'.

The bride of Christ, the New Church, shall live in the *presence of the King*. Only 5 of the 10 virgins mentioned in St. Matthew 25, made it in to see the bridegroom. The 5 wise virgins carried the oil in their lamps plus they had extra oil. The 5 foolish virgins made no preparation for the next level. They intended to live off the wise virgins oil, they could not be bothered to pay their own price to get their own oil. Only those who were prepared made it in. They paid the price for what they had, it had been costly. They had been set apart, separated and consecrated for ministry. The oil which they carried would be transferred to the inside of their vessel, once they met with the bridegroom. The oil which also represents the Holy Spirit, would possess them and they would be completed ready for full time ministry. Vessels of the Lord.

**Wrought Gold**

Wrought Gold speaks of '*Spiritual Purity*'.

The attitude of consistently conforming to the will of God so that Christ can delight himself in the bride and her beauty. Beauty speaks of spiritual glory and spiritual beauty. Humility a yielded will and yielded vessel. Humble, meek and obedient, submissiveness, honour reverence, and love. Right here Christ will rest dwell in our submissiveness willingness, truthfulness humility and obedience. He will 'habitate' us.

It's an atmosphere of *praise*, red hot praise that has been created to encircle, embrace and entertain the presence and glory of the Lord. It's a wealthy moist atmosphere. A creative atmosphere of creative miracles. Signs and wonders and the healing power of God.

The Church is to be subject to Christ, as the bride is to her bridegroom, wife to husband and is to call him Lord as Sarah called Abraham. We must worship Christ The Lord for this is the will of God, that all men should honour the Son.

Eve was presented to Adam. Genesis 2:22. The bride of Christ will be presented to Christ by the 'Father'. Eve represents the bride of Christ. Adam represents the head of the Church, the husband, Christ Jesus our Lord and Saviour, the Bridegroom. Eve, a finished and completed work, product image of the man and they twain become one flesh. One in spirit, one in mind and one in love and agreement.

'Esther' speaks of the Church in the 'final hour' spiritually pure, so much so, that Christ had to ask her, 'what is your request? He was delighted in her. Esther had come through her training period, her past, her abuse, dead issues, current issue, trials and errors and was now made whole again and pure, submissive, honest true to herself and to God and was now ready for the next level. Esther 9:12/7:2 & Esther 5:6.

God is calling his bride to 'arise to the **purpose** and **call** of God. The women of God shall arise in this final hour to their destiny and the will of God shall be fulfilled. God is going to use women in a mighty way to bring back His glory. Our gift will make room for us in areas that may not have been penetrated before!

# CHAPTER 18

## VOW OF ACCEPTANCE

As I bring this book to a close, I would like to share with you one final thing. I have just come through another **hard** trial. One of those where God asks you to do something and instead of going the way God told you to go, you tried to avoid that route completely so you don't have to deal with certain things and particular issues that need to be dealt with in your life. So the confusion is caused initially by disobeying or going against the instructions given.

God does not only interrupt your life or plans once only, but He does it again and again, to fit into His programme and schedule. He will shut doors that no one can open because He is pushing and provoking you to do His will. You can run but you can't hide.

Now that I have come to a place of *total surrender* in my heart and in my spirit, and true repentance has taken place, the Lord has asked that I would make a *'vow of acceptance'* of his will for my life! I encourage you to do so too. When you make that vow, all the doorways and avenues that Satan was allowed to operate through are shut in the spirit realm because there is no room for him to manoeuvre now. Say yes from the heart and from your spirit. Your vow will seal the illegal open doors.

Make a commitment to God to give up, throw your hands up in the air and come on down boldly to the mercy seat, so that you may obtain grace now. It's God's way or no way. Make the right choice, say yes to the Lord, and your tomorrow, your future will be bright. Silver or Gold, you choose. The longer you take, the harder the way becomes. Choose Gold, the precious things of God. God's chosen desire for you. You have been especially elected for this, because you are chosen by God.

There is a *rainbow of promise* awaiting you, so come on let's choose Gold. God is waiting to bless you *abundantly!*

ISBN 1-4120-5569-5

9 781412 055697